HONDA TWINS
Owners
Workshop
Manual

by Jeff Clew

(with additional material on the CB 200 model by Stewart Wilkins)

Models covered

122 cc	CB 125	
161 cc	CB 160	
174 cc	CB 175	CD 175
198 cc	CB 200	

All models from 1964

ISBN 900550 67 8

Printed in England   *(067 - 10B3)*

HAYNES PUBLISHING GROUP
SPARKFORD YEOVIL SOMERSET ENGLAND
distributed in the USA by
HAYNES PUBLICATIONS INC
861 LAWRENCE DRIVE
NEWBURY PARK
CALIFORNIA 91320
USA

Acknowledgements

Grateful thanks are due to Honda (UK) Limited for the technical assistance given so freely whilst this manual was being prepared, and for permission to reproduce their drawings, Richard Winslade provided the CB175K6, the model which was used for the photographic sequences, and Bryan Goss Motor Cycles of Yeovil supplied the necessary spare parts used during the rebuild. Brian Horsfall assisted with the dismantling and rebuilding sequences and devised the various ingenious methods for overcoming the lack of service tools. Les Brazier arranged and took the photographs; Tim Parker edited the text. We are particularly grateful to I. S. Cox of Darlington, who supplied much useful information about the machines covered in this manual.

We should also like to acknowledge the help of the Avon Rubber Company who kindly supplied the illustrations that apply to tyre fitting and NGK Spark Plug (UK) Limited for the provision of Spark plug photographs.

The cover photograph was arranged through the courtesy of Vincent and Jerrom Ltd, Taunton.

About this manual

The author of this manual has the conviction that the only way in which a meaningful and easy to follow text can be written is first to do the work himself, under conditions similar to those found in the average household. As a result, the hands seen in the photographs are those of the author. Even the machine photographed was not new; an example that had covered several thousand miles was selected so that the conditions encountered would be similar to those found by the average rider. Unless specially mentioned, and therefore considered essential, Honda service tools have not been used. There is invariably some alternative means of slackening or removing some vital component when service tools are not available and risk of damage has to be avoided at all costs.

Each of the six chapters is divided into numbered sections. Within the sections are numbered paragraphs. In consequence. cross reference throughout this manual is both straightforward and logical. When a reference is made 'See Section 5.12' it means Section 5, paragraph 12 in the same Chapter. If another chapter were meant, the text would read 'See Chapter 2, Section 5.12'. All photographs are captioned with a section/paragraph number to which they refer and are always relevant to the chapter text adjacent.

Figure numbers (usually line illustrations) appear in numerical order, within a given chapter. Fig 1.1. therefore refers to the first figure in Chapter 1. Left hand and right hand descriptions of the machines and their component parts refer to the right and left of a given machine when the rider is seated normally.

Whilst every care is taken to ensure that the information in this manual is correct no liability can be accepted by the authors or publishers for loss, damage or injury, caused by any errors in or omissions from the information given.

Modifications to the Honda 125, 160 and 175 cc range

More than ten years have passed since the first lightweight Honda twin reached the UK market, a period during which many design changes and detail improvements have been made. The early models had the camshaft drive chain mounted on the extreme left hand side of the engine unit and are not included in this manual. Later models, covered fully by this manual, have a different arrangement in which the camshaft drive is mounted within a tunnel between the two cylinders. Models have been available either as a touring or a sports motor cycle

All significant design changes are mentioned in the main text under a separate heading where appropriate. It will be appreciated that some variants of the models included in this manual were supplied to countries other than the UK, but in the main these differences are either 'cosmetic' or relate to the lighting equipment, which has to meet the statutory requirements of the country into which the machine is imported.

Contents

Model CB 175

Model CD 175

Introduction
to the Honda 125, 160, 175 and 200cc twins

Although the Honda twin made its first European debut at the Amsterdam Show in 1959, it was not until 1964 that the first lightweight twins became available in the UK. These models, designated C92 (touring) and CB92 (sports) formed the spearhead of many lightweight models that were to follow. Each could readily be identified by the pronounced 'rectangular' styling, which was applied even to the headlamps, rear suspension units and other cycle parts. Frames and forks were constructed from steel pressings.

The reception which these and the other models in the Honda range were given was nothing short of dramatic. Within a very short period of time the Japanese models outsold all other machines of similar capacity, making Honda a household word almost overnight.

All of the twin cylinder models are fitted with a chain driven overhead camshaft engine. In the original design, the camshaft drive was taken from the extreme left hand side of the engine unit, but more recently design changes have included the repositioning of the camshaft drive between the two cylinders, where it can operate under conditions of improved temperature stability. Early engines have a marked inclination of the cylinder barrels, although this cannot be interpreted as a reliable means of determining the position of the camshaft drive.

The CB125 models had only a comparatively short run in the UK; of the 160 cc and 175 cc models, only the latter are still available. These models have proved particularly suitable for the learner rider who requires good performance but is restricted to a machine of less than 250 cc capacity until the driving test is passed. They also find favour with other discriminating riders who prefer a lightweight machine capable of good performance with low running costs.

During February 1974 a new CB200 model was added to the range. It is similar in many respects to the CB175 model but is more than just a 'stretched' version.

Model dimensions

Dimensions	CB125 and CB160	CB175	CD175	CB200
Overall length (in)	76¾ (1974 mm)	77.8 (1975 mm)	77.95 (1980 mm)	76.18 (1935 mm)
Overall width (in)	29.31 (745 mm)	29.31 (745 mm)	29.52 (750 mm)	28.34 (720 mm)
Overall height (in)	39 (990 mm)	40.0 (1015 mm)	40.15 (1020 mm)	41.73 (1060 mm)
Wheelbase (in)	50.25 (1277 mm)	50.2 (1275 mm)	50.39 (1280 mm)	50.78 (1290 mm)
Weight (lb)	280 (127 kg)	299.9 (136 kg)	271.2 (123 kg)	291 (132 kg)

Ordering spare parts

When ordering spare parts for any Honda it is advisable to deal direct with an official Honda agent who should be able to supply most of the parts ex-stock. Parts cannot be obtained from Honda (UK) Limited direct; all orders must be routed via an approved agent, even if the parts required are not held in stock.

Always quote the engine and frame numbers in full, particularly if parts are required for any of the earlier models. The frame number is stamped on the left hand side of the steering head, reading upwards from the base. The engine number is stamped on the left hand side of the upper crankcase, immediately to the rear of the left hand cylinder barrel. It is advisable to quote the 'K' number that follows the catalogue number of the machine because this denotes any minor modifications that have been incorporated during the production run of any particular model. Lastly, it is advisable to make note of the colour scheme, especially if any cycle parts are to be included in the order.

Use only parts of genuine Honda manufacture. Pattern parts are available, some of which originate from Japan and are packed in boxes of similar design to the manufacturer's originals. Pattern parts do not necessarily make a satisfactory replacement, even if there is an initial price advantage. Many cases are on record where reduced life or sudden failure has occurred, to the detriment of performance and reliability.

Some of the more expendable parts such as spark plugs, bulbs, tyres, oils and greases etc., can be obtained from accessory shops and motor factors, who have convenient opening hours, charge lower prices and can often be found not far from home. It is also possible to obtain parts on a Mail Order basis from a number of specialists who advertise regularly in the motor cycle magazines.

Engine number

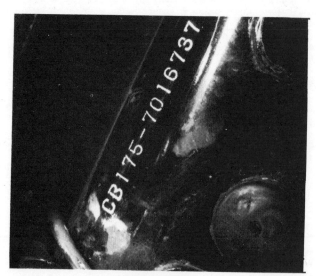

Frame number

Routine Maintenance

Periodic routine maintenance is a continuous process that commences immediately the machine is used and continues until the machine is no longer fit for use. It must be carried out at specific mileage recordings, or on a calendar basis if the machine is not used regularly, whichever the soonest. Maintenance should be regarded as an insurance policy, to help keep the machine in the peak of condition and to ensure long, trouble-free use. It has the additional benefit of giving early warning of any faults that may develop and will act as a safety check, to the obvious advantage of both rider and machine alike.

The various maintenance tasks are described, under their respective mileage and calendar headings. Accompanying diagrams are provided, where necessary. It should be remembered that the interval between the various maintenance tasks serves only as a guide. As the machine gets older, is driven hard or is used under particularly adverse conditions, it is advisable to reduce the interval between each check.

If a specific item is mentioned but not described in detail, it will be covered fully in the appropriate chapter. No special tools are required for the normal routine maintenance tasks. Those contained in the tool kit supplied with every new machine will suffice, but if they are not available, the tools found in the average household will make an adequate substitute.

Weekly or every 200 miles

Check the oil level of the engine/gear unit. The filler cap has an integral dipstick; readings should be taken with the cap resting in the mouth of the filler orifice, but NOT screwed home. Use only the recommended grades of oil.

Check the tyre pressures. Always check when the tyres are cool, using a pressure gauge of known accuracy.

Check the level of electrolyte in the battery. Use only distilled water to top up, unless there has been a spillage of acid. Do not overfill.

Give the whole machine a close visual inspection for loose nuts and fittings, frayed control cables etc. Make sure the lights, horn traffic indicators and speedometer function correctly. Remember the efficient working of most of these components is a statutory requirement.

Check, and if necessary, adjust both brakes.

Monthly or every 1000 miles

Complete each of the checks listed in the Weekly/200 mile service, then attend to the following items:

Change the engine oil.
Adjust the final drive chain and lubricate, if necessary.
Check the tightness of the cylinder head bolts, the exhaust pipe clamps and the carburettor tops.

Six monthly or every 3000 miles

Complete all of the checks listed in the Weekly/200 mile service and then the following:

Remove the spark plugs, clean and adjust the points gap. If the electrodes are badly eroded or the insulators badly fouled, both plugs should be renewed.

Check and, if necessary, adjust the contact breaker points. Verify the accuracy of the ignition timing AFTER the points gaps have been set.

Check the valve clearances with the engine COLD and adjust as necessary.

Check also the tension of the camshaft drive chain.

Remove and clean the air filter element. If the element is damp or oily, it must be replaced.

Remove the filter bowl from the petrol tap and clean both the bowl and the filter gauze. Check that the fuel lines are free from sediment.

Check the clutch operation and re-adjust as necessary.

Remove and clean the final drive chain, lubricating it thoroughly before replacement. Check the condition of both the gearbox and the rear wheel sprockets.

Make sure both carburettors are clean and adjusted correctly. Check that they are synchronised correctly.

Yearly or every 6000 miles

Complete all the checks under the weekly, monthly and six monthly headings, then carry out the following additional tasks:

Clean the oil filter.
Replace the air cleaner element.
Remove both wheels and check the condition of the brake shoes.
Change the oil content of the front forks.
Check and if necessary adjust the steering head bearings.
Check the action of the steering head lock.

NOTE: No specific mention has been made of tyre wear since it is assumed the rider will maintain a regular check. Apart from the statutory requirement relating to the minimum depth of tread permissible, a tyre that has cracked or damaged sidewalls should also be replaced immediately, in the interests of safety.

8

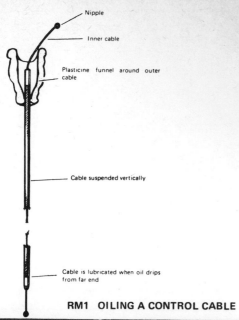

Nipple
Inner cable
Plasticine funnel around outer cable
Cable suspended vertically
Cable is lubricated when oil drips from far end

RM1 OILING A CONTROL CABLE

RM4 OIL REAR CHAIN REGULARLY WITH ENGINE OIL

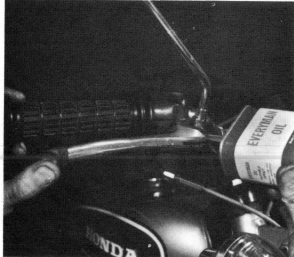

RM2 OIL LEVER PIVOTS AND CABLE NIPPLES

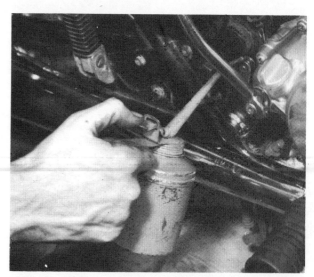

RM5 TRUNNIONS ON REAR BRAKE ROD ARE OFTEN OVERLOOKED

RM3 CHECK ENGINE OIL LEVEL FREQUENTLY

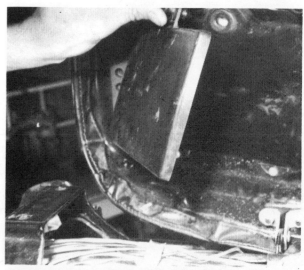

RM6 MOULDING UNDER DUAL SEAT HOLDS OWNER MANUAL

Quick glance routine maintenance adjustments and capacities

Contact breaker gaps	0.012 in - 0.016 in	
Spark plugs	NGK D-8HS	
Spark plug gaps	0.024 in - 0.028 in	
Fuel tank capacity	**2.2 Imp gallons (12 litres)**	CB175/CD175
	2.3 Imp gallons (10.5 litres)	CB160/CB125
Engine/gearbox oil capacity	2.6 Imp pints (1.5 litres)	CB175/CD175
	1.76 Imp pints (1 litre)	CB160/CB125
Tyre pressures	Front lbs 26 psi Rear lbs 28 psi *	

* Increase rear tyre pressure to lb 34 psi when a pillion passenger is carried

Recommended lubricants

Engine/gearbox	Castrol GTX	2.6 Imp pints (1.5 litres) CB175/CD175 1.76 Imp pints (1.0 litre) CB160/CB125
Grease nipples	Castrol LM Grease	
Control cables	Castrol Everyman Oil	
Telescopic forks	Castrol TQF	4.7 - 5.1 fluid ounces (140 - 150 cc per leg)

Line drawings

Chapter 1 Engine, Clutch and Gearbox

Contents

Specifications

Model	CB125	CB160	CB175/CD175
Engine		Twin cylinder overhead camshaft	
Cylinder head		Aluminium alloy	
Cylinder block		Aluminium alloy	
Bore	44 mm	50 mm	52 mm
Stroke	41 mm	41 mm	41 mm
Cubic capacity	124 cc	161 cc	174 cc
Compression ratio	9 : 1	8.5 : 1	9 : 1
Bhp	15 @ 10,500 rpm	16.5 @ 10,000 rpm	20 @ 10,500 rpm (CB175) 17 @ 10,000 rpm (CD175)
Pistons			
Type		Aluminium alloy	
Oversizes available		+ 0.25 mm (0.010 in) + 0.50 mm (0.020 in) + 0.75 mm (0.030 in) + 1.0 mm (0.040 in)	

Piston rings

Number per piston	Two compression, one oil control		
End gap	0.006 in - 0.015 in compression rings		
	0.004 in - 0.011 in oil control rings		
Groove clearance	0.0005 in - 0.0017 in	0.0016 in - 0.0028 in	
	(all rings)	(top rings)	
		0.0004 in - 0.0016 in	
		(2nd and oil)	

Cylinders

Bore wear limit	44.1 mm	50.1 mm	52.1 mm

Valves

Valve stem diameter - inlet	5.48 - 5.49 mm (0.2157 - 0.2161 in)
Valve stem diameter - exhaust	5.46 - 5.47 mm (0.2149 - 0.2153 in)
Wear limit - inlet	5.42 mm (0.2193 in)
Wear limit - exhaust	5.40 mm (0.2126 in)

Valve springs

Free length - inner	28.6 mm (1.1 in)	31.8 mm (1.2520 in)
Free length - outer	36.2 mm (1.4 in)	30.2 mm (1.1890 in)
Wear limit - inner	Not available	30.6 mm (1.2047 in)
Wear limit - outer	Not available	27.9 mm (1.0984 in)

Valve clearances (engine cold) ... ...   0.002 in (0.05 mm)

Valve timing (at 1.1 mm lift)

Inlet opens	5º BTDC	Data not available
Inlet closes	30º ABDC	for CB175/CD175
Exhaust opens	30º BBDC	models
Exhaust closes	5º ATDC	

Clutch

Number of inserted plates	Five		
Number of plain plates	Five		
Thickness of inserted plates	3.5 mm (1.14 in)	3.5 mm (1.14 in)	3.0 mm (1.118 in)
Wear limit	3.4 mm	3.4 mm	2.9 mm (1.114 in)
Springs - free length	34.9 mm		35.5 mm (1.3976 in)
Springs - wear limit	34.6 mm		34.2 mm (1.3465 in)

Torque wrench settings

Cylinder head nuts	11 - 14 lb f ft
Automatic ignition advance unit	5.8 - 8.7 lb f ft
Carburettors to cylinder heads	5.0 - 6.1 lb f ft
Crankcase covers	5.8 - 8.7 lb f ft
Crankcase - 8 mm bolts	16.6 - 20.2 lb f ft
- 6 mm bolts	5.7 - 8.6 lb f ft
Generator rotor	11.5 - 12.2 lb f ft
Primary drive pinion	47.0 - 57.8 lb f ft
Final drive sprocket	13.7 - 17.3 lb f ft

1 General description

The engine unit fitted to the Honda CB125, CB160, CB175 and CD175 models is of the parallel twin cylinder type with valves operated by a chain driven overhead camshaft. The camshaft is located within the cylinder head casting and the chain drive operates through a cast-in tunnel between the two cylinders. Adjustment is effected by means of a tensioner.

All engine/gear units are of aluminium alloy construction, with the crankcase arranged to divide horizontally. The cylinders of the CB160 engine are angled at 30º from the vertical; all other models have only an 8º inclination. A flywheel magneto generator of the AC type is mounted on the left hand side of the engine unit; the clutch assembly is located on the right hand side, behind a domed aluminium alloy cover. The exhaust system is of the twin downswept type, each pipe having its own silencer. All models are fitted with a kickstarter; an electric starter is fitted to provide an alternative and more convenient method of starting the engine.

Lubrication is effected by a plunger type oil pump, driven by an eccentric pump rod behind the clutch. Oil from the crankcase chamber is fed via a centrifugal oil filter to all the crankshaft bearings through an oilway in the upper crankcase. Both big end bearings are lubricated by force feed from the oil pump. An additional feed from the upper crankcase carries oil to the cylinder barrels and cylinder heads and to the camshaft and camshaft rocker arms. The excess returns via the tunnel around the camshaft chain, to lubricate the chain before draining into the crankcase. A quite separate feed from the upper crankcase enters the gearbox unit to ensure this too is adequately lubricated.

All engines are built in-unit with the gearbox. This means that when the engine is dismantled the clutch and gearbox are dismantled too. This task is made easy by arranging the crankcase to separate in the horizontal plane.

2 Operations with engine/gearbox in frame

1 It is not necessary to remove the engine unit from the frame unless the crankshaft assembly and/or the gearbox bearings or pinions require attention. Most operations can be accomplished

with the engine in place, such as:

a) Removal and replacement of the flywheel magneto generator.
b) Removal and replacement of the clutch.
c) Removal and replacement of the starter motor.

2   When several operations have to be undertaken simultaneously, it will probably be advantageous to remove the complete engine/gear unit from the frame, an operation that should take approximately an hour. This will give the advantage of better access and more working space.

3   Operations with engine/gearbox removed

1   Removal and replacement of the cylinder head casting
2   Removal and replacement of the cylinder block and pistons.
3   Removal and replacement of the main bearings.
4   Removal and replacement of the crankshaft assembly.
5   Removal and replacement of the gear cluster, selectors and gearbox main bearings.

4   Method of engine/gearbox removal

As described previously, the engine and gearbox are built in-unit and it is necessary to remove the unit complete in order to gain access to either component. Separation is accomplished after the engine unit has been removed and refitting cannot take place until the crankcases have been reassembled.

5   Removing the engine/gearbox unit

1   Place the machine on the centre stand and make sure it is standing firmly. Remove the crankcase drain plug and drain oil from the crankcase. Approximately 1¾ to 2½ pints will drain off, depending on the model.
2   Disconnect the battery by removing the positive lead. The battery is located beneath the dual seat, which will hinge to the left to give access, or in the case of the CD175 model, behind the right hand cover.
3   Drain and remove the petrol tank. The tank will not drain completely until the rubber tube connecting the underside of both halves of the tank is disconnected. Have a container ready to avoid spillage. The tank is retained solely by rubber pads that abut against frame members, and by a rubber sleeve that fits over a projection at the end of the tank, except in the case of the CB125 and CB160 models. These latter models have a rubber bushed retaining bolt that passes through two small lugs welded to the extreme lower end of the tank.
4   Remove the finned clips from both exhaust pipes. They are retained by two nuts and washers on studs threaded into the exhaust port surrounds. Note that each clip has two split clamps within to grip the pipe.
5   Withdraw the two bolts and spring washers that retain each silencer to the pillion footrest bracket. They thread into captive nuts. Some models have a variation of this fixing method, depending on the type of silencer fitted.
6   Release the silencers complete with exhaust pipes by twisting them through 90° so that they will clear the gap between the footrests and the frame. Since it is necessary to remove the footrests next, this action can be deferred if there is risk of scratching the plated surfaces. On the CB160 models with the spine-type frame, the footrests bolt direct to the underside of the lower crankcase. On the full frame models (CB125K3, CD175 and CB175) they bolt direct to threaded lugs welded to the underside of each lower frame tube.
7   Remove the final drive cover from the left hand side of the engine unit. This is retained by three crosshead screws and will necessitate the use of an impact screwdriver if the screws have not been removed previously. Avoid damaging the heads at all

costs, otherwise the screws will prove almost impossible to remove. Detach the clutch cable by raising the operating arm with a screwdriver and detaching the nipple.
8   Remove the final drive chain by withdrawing the spring link. This task is made easier if the spring link is positioned on the rear wheel sprocket, so that the chain is held in the sprocket teeth during the removal operation. On CD175 models remove the chain sprocket without separating the chain. This will save having to remove the chaincase.
9   Detach the plug leads from both cylinders and tuck them out of the way. Remove the tachometer drive cable by detaching the chromium plated cover on the right hand cylinder head (one crosshead screw) and then removing the crosshead screw that holds the cable in position. The cable will pull out when the screw is withdrawn. Note that a union nut fitting is employed in the case of the CB125 and CB160 models, simplifying disconnection.
10   Remove the kickstarter and the gear change pedal. Both are retained on their respective shafts by means of a pinch bolt that tightens the lever or pedal around the splines. Check that both shaft and lever or pedal are marked with a centre punch, to ensure they are subsequently replaced at the same angle.
11   Detach the air cleaner hoses from the intakes of both carburettors. They are a push-on fit. Remove the condenser or disconnect the leads (simpler). (CB175 and CD175 models only). Unscrew both carburettor tops and lift out the slide and needle assemblies. Tie these to a nearby member, to avoid damage.
12   Disconnect the various electrical connections. The snap connectors are usually grouped near the frame spine, secured by a plastic clip. Disconnect the starter motor cable either from the solenoid under the dual seat or from the starter motor body itself. It will be necessary to thread the cable away from the engine so that it does not hinder removal of the engine unit.
13   Detach the engine mounting bolts (9, full frame models CB125K3, CD175 and CB175 and 6, model CB160). Note: The top front engine bolt of the CD175 and CB175 models may prove a little difficult to remove due to the close proximity of the starter motor.
14   Lift the engine unit out from the right hand side, raising it both forwards and upwards. By virtue of the frame construction, the CB160 engine can be removed more easily since there is no front down tube to impede movement. Extra care must be taken to support the engine when the mounting bolts are removed. Although none of the engine units are unduly heavy, it is advisable to have a second person available during the removal operation to help with the initial engine removal and to steady the frame and cycle parts as the engine is lifted clear.

5.2 Disconnect battery by removing both leads

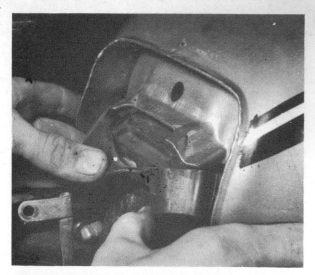

5.3 Slip rubber sleeve from lip on end of tank

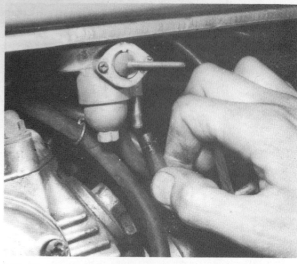

5.3a Remove feed pipe from petrol tap

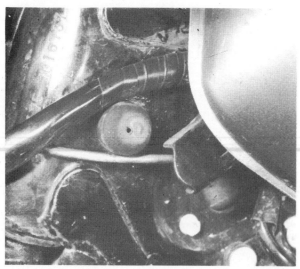

5.3b Channels engage with frame rubbers at nose of tank

5.3c Tank can be lifted clear from rear end

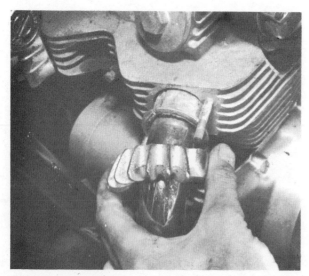

5.4 Finned clips retain clamps around exhaust pipes

5.5 Forward bolt passes through frame extension

5.5a Rear bolt passes through base of pillion footrest

5.6 Twist exhaust system to free from footrests

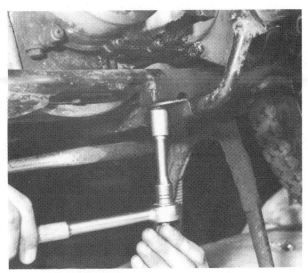

5.6a Footrests bolt to underside of frame on 175 cc models

5.7 Final drive cover is retained by three screws

5.7a Detach clutch cable from operating arm

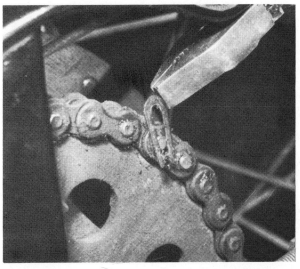

5.8 Position spring link in sprocket to make detachment easy

5.9 Plated cover seals off tachometer drive (CB175)

5.9a Crosshead screw retains tachometer cable in drive ...

5.9b Cable will pull out when screw is released

5.10 Kickstarter is retained on splines by pinch bolt

5.10a Gear change lever is retained in similar fashion

5.11 Detach air cleaner hoses from carburettor intakes

5.11a Remove also carburettor tops

5.11b Condenser is mounted under cylinder head cover nut

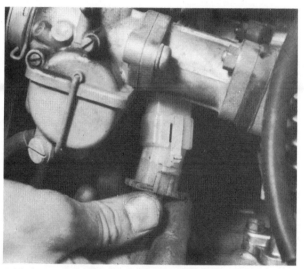

5.12 Snap connectors make disconnection easy

5.12a Disconnect starter motor cable from solenoid or ...

5.12b ... starter motor body

5.13 Engine is mounted at cylinder head (CB175 and CD175) ...

5.13a ... short engine plates at front of engine ...

5.13b ... at rear base of crankcase

5.13c Upper rear engine bolt acts as earthing point

5.14 Lift out engine from right hand side

6 Dismantling the engine and gearbox - general

1 Before commencing work on the engine unit, the external surfaces should be cleaned thoroughly. A motor cycle engine has very little protection from road grit and other foreign matter which sooner or later will find its way into the dismantled engine if this simple precaution is not fulfilled.

2 One of the proprietary cleaning compounds such as Gunk or Jizer can be used to good effect, especially if the compound is first allowed to penetrate the film of grease and oil before it is washed away. When washing down make sure that the water cannot enter the carburettors or the electrical system, particularly now that these parts are more exposed.

3 Collect together a good set of tools including a set of metric spanners and a screwdriver with a crosshead bit of the correct size. If the engine has not been dismantled previously, it is advisable to either purchase or borrow an impact screwdriver. This will avoid damaging the heads of the crosshead screws, used for engine assembly, most of which will be very tight. If an impact screwdriver is not available, it is often possible to use a crosshead screwdriver fitted with a 'T' handle as a substitute. Work on a clean surface and have a supply of clean, lint-free rag available.

4 Never use force to remove any stubborn part unless specific mention is made of this requirement in the text. There is invariably good reason why a part is difficult to remove, often because the dismantling operation has been tackled in the wrong sequence.

5 Dismantling will be made easier if a simple engine stand is constructed that will correspond with the engine mounting points. This arrangement will permit the complete unit to be clamped rigidly to the workbench, leaving both hands free for the dismantling operation.

7 Dismantling the engine and gearbox - removing the carburettor(s)

1 Each carburettor is retained to its respective cylinder head by two nuts and washers on the ends of the holding down studs that extend from each intake flange. Remove these nuts and washers and draw the carburettors off as a pair; they will be joined by the link of the cold starting choke. Take care not to lose the O ring seals from each carburettor flange and draw the gaskets and heat insulators off the holding down studs. The CD175 model has only a single carburettor.

2 Place the carburettor(s) aside for further attention. They are

very easily damaged if handled roughly. If desired, they can be separated by withdrawing the split pin through one of the choke operating levers, so that the choke link can be detached.

7.1 Pull off both carburettors together with choke linkage

8 Dismantling the engine and gearbox - removing the cylinder head and block

1 Before commencing to slacken the bolts that retain the cylinder head cover in position, remove the breather tube attached to the rear of the casting. Then slacken in a diagonal sequence the seven dome nuts that retain the cover in position (one has been removed previously to free the condenser, CB175 and CD175 models only). Before the cover can be lifted off, it is necessary to slacken and remove a small hexagon bolt, hidden within a forward facing lug used for the cylinder cover mounting bolt. The cover can then be lifted away, exposing the camshaft, camshaft drive chain and the rocker gear.

2 Remove the circular generator cover retained by three crosshead screws. This will enable the generator rotor to be turned by placing a spanner on the retaining nut so that the spring link in the camshaft chain is positioned at the top of the camshaft drive sprocket. It is advisable to attach a piece of thin wire or string to each end of the camshaft drive chain when the spring link is removed, so that the chain does not fall through the tunnel into the crankcase. If the chain is supported in this fashion whilst the cylinder head is raised, the wire or string will thread through the tunnel, permitting the cylinder head to be lifted away completely.

3 To release the cylinder block, first slacken off the camshaft chain tensioner. Then unscrew and remove the single bolt at the rear of the base of the cylinder block. The cylinder block is now free to be lifted away from the crankcase, taking care to support the pistons and rings as they emerge from the cylinder bores.

4 It is advisable to pad the mouth of the crankcase as soon as the cylinder block is raised a little, especially if a bottom end overhaul is not contemplated. This simple precaution will prevent foreign matter from dropping into the crankcase, or particles of broken piston ring if damage of this nature is suspected.

5 The camshaft chain can again be fed through the tunnel whilst the free ends are retained by wire or string. There is no necessity to remove it completely, unless the crankcase has to be separated, in which case it is best detached completely.

6 The camshaft chain tensioner rod and spring will be displaced as the cylinder block is lifted, due to the fact that the adjuster has been slackened off.

8.1 Pull off breather pipe from cylinder head cover

8.1a Do not overlook bolt hidden in mounting lug

8.1b Lift off cover to expose rockers and camshaft

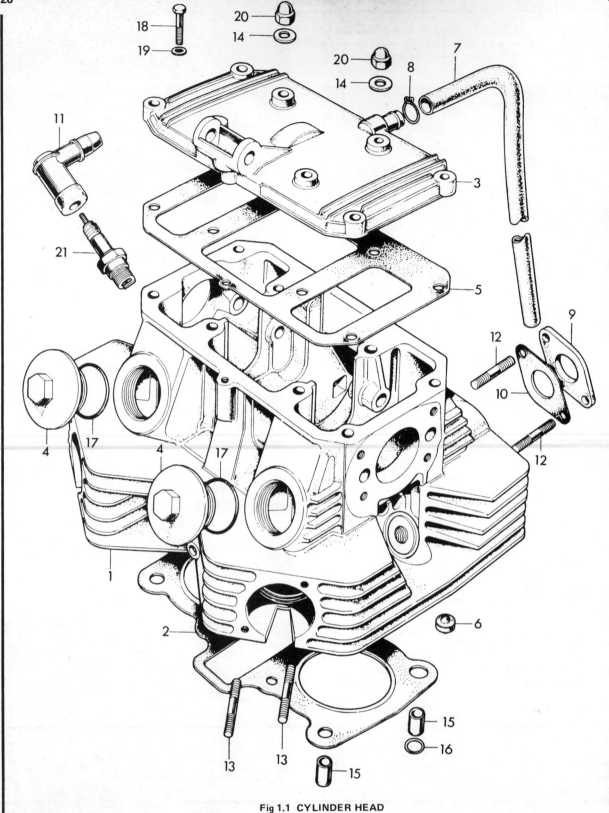

Fig 1.1 CYLINDER HEAD

1 Cylinder head
2 Cylinder head gasket
3 Cylinder head cover
4 Tappet adjusting cap - 4 off
5 Cylinder cover gasket
6 Rubber insert
7 Breather pipe

8 Breather pipe clip
9 Carburettor heat insulator -
   2 off, all models except
   CD175
10 Carburettor insulator gasket -
   2 off, all models except
   CD175

11 Plug cap - suppressor type -
   2 off
12 Carburettor mounting studs -
   4 off (2 off, CD175 model)
13 Exhaust pipe mounting
   studs - 4 off
14 Flat washer - 8 off

15 Dowel pins - 4 off
16 O ring - 2 off
17 O ring - 4 off
18 Bolt
19 Flat washer
20 Acorn nut - 8 off
21 Spark plug - 2 off

8.2 Reassembly is easier if timing is aligned whilst dismantling

8.2a Remove spring link at top of camshaft sprocket

8.2b Use wire to hold camshaft chain whilst lifting cylinder head

8.3 Before lifting cylinder block, slacken off chain tensioner

8.3a Single bolt at rear of block must be removed, then ...

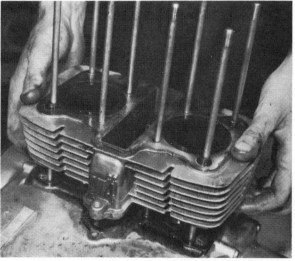

8.3b ... block can be lifted off crankcase

8.6   Chain tensioner bolts to top of crankcase (shown with pistons removed)

9   Dismantling the engine and gearbox - removing the pistons and piston rings

1   Remove both circlips from each piston boss and discard them. Circlips should never be re-used if risk of displacement is to be obviated.
2   Using a drift of the correct diameter, tap each gudgeon pin out of position whilst supporting the piston rod and connecting rod. When the gudgeon pin is displaced sufficiently, the piston will lift off the connecting rod, complete with rings. Mark each piston INSIDE the skirt so that it is replaced in the same position.
3   If the gudgeon pins prove to be a tight fit in the piston bosses, the pistons should be warmed first to expand the metal. A convenient method is to place a rag soaked in hot water on each piston crown. Do not use excessive force to displace the pins on any account for there is grave risk of bending the connecting rods.
4   No separate small end bearing is fitted to the connecting rods. Each rod, which is of a hard wearing material, is bored direct to accept the gudgeon pin.
5   To remove the piston rings, spread the ends apart with the thumbs, sufficiently for the rings to be lifted off the pistons. This is a very delicate operation which must be accomplished with great care. The piston rings are brittle and will break easily if mishandled.
6   If the piston rings are to be re-used, keep them separate and in their correct order, so that they are replaced on the piston to which they were originally fitted. Both compression rings are chromium plated and have a slight taper - the uppermost surface is marked 'top' to aid replacement. The oil control ring has what is known as a Parkerised finish. If replacements are fitted, they must correspond to this specification.

9.1   Remove and discard circlips

10   Dismantling the engine and gearbox - removing the left hand crankcase cover

1   Remove the left hand crankcase cover, retained by nine crosshead screws. If the cover has not been removed previously, an impact screwdriver will be needed.
2   Release the clip that retains the generator wiring harness grommet to the crankcase and the green wire connection. The outer cover can now be drawn away from the crankcase with the stator coil assembly and wiring harness attached. Take care not to misplace the two locating dowels.

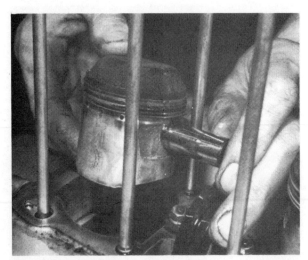

9.2   Displace gudgeon pins to free pistons

10.1   Left hand crankcase cover is retained by nine screws

11 Dismantling the engine and gearbox - removing the starter motor and generator rotor

1 When the left hand crankcase cover has been removed, access is available to the starter motor drive and the generator rotor. To remove the starter motor, unscrew the two crosshead screws that retain the starter motor to the right hand side of the upper crankcase.

2 The starter motor sprocket will pull off the splines of the starter motor shaft; it has no retainer. If the chain is of the endless type, the starter motor can be withdrawn from the crankcase casting. It may be necessary to give a few light taps with a rawhide mallet because the boss of the motor is a tight fit in the aperture of the casting, especially if the starter motor has not previously been disturbed. When the sprocket is free, the chain can be lifted from the larger sprocket, behind the generator rotor.

3 Some machines have a chain fitted with a spring link which makes disconnection easier.

4 Remove the sprocket guide that is retained by a single crosshead screw. This guide retains the larger sprocket in position behind the generator rotor.

5 The generator rotor is a keyed fit onto the tapered end of the crankshaft. To expose the extractor thread in the centre of the rotor, remove the centre bolt and washer.

6 If the Honda extractor tool is not available, the rear wheel spindle makes an excellent substitute. It is of the same diameter and has the same thread. When it is screwed into the extractor thread and tightened it will abut against the end of the crankshaft and pull the rotor off the taper.

7 The starter motor free running clutch is contained within the rear of the generator rotor. Refer to Chapter 6.8 for further details. The larger of the starter motor sprockets is a push fit over the crankshaft, behind the rotor, and can be lifted off.

8 A starter motor is not fitted to the UK imported CD175 model.

11.1 Two crosshead screws retain the starter motor to the crankcase

11.2 Pull the starter motor sprocket off its splines

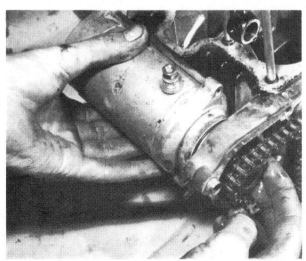

11.2a Withdraw the starter motor backwards at the same time

11.2b Lift off the chain from the larger sprocket

11.4 Remove the sprocket guide

11.5 Remove centre bolt of rotor to expose extractor thread

11.6 Rear wheel spindle makes excellent rotor extractor

12 Dismantling the engine and gearbox - removing the final drive sprocket

1 The final drive sprocket has a splined centre that matches with the splines on the end of the gearbox layshaft. It is retained by a plate and two bolts that thread into the sprocket.

2 It is advantageous to remove the sprocket at this stage, since further dismantling work will necessitate working with the engine unit right hand side uppermost.

11.7 Starter motor driven sprocket pulls off crankshaft

12.1 Final drive sprocket is retained by two bolts and a plate

13 Dismantling the engine and gearbox - removing the centrifugal oil filter

1 Reposition the engine unit with the right hand side uppermost and remove the oil filter outer cover, then the right hand crankcase cover. This latter cover has eleven crosshead screws and when withdrawn will expose the centrifugal oil filter and the clutch.

2 Remove the oil filter cover by withdrawing the crosshead screw recessed into the centre. The screw head may be hidden completely if oil has collected inside the recess. When the screw is withdrawn, the cover can be lifted away with a pair of pliers.

3 The body of the filter is secured to the end of the crankshaft by means of a sleeve nut which is extremely difficult to unscrew without the appropriate Honda service tool. A close fitting socket spanner can be used as a substitute, placing a shaped strip of welding rod across two of the sleeve nut slots before the socket is tapped into position. The wire strip provides sufficient grip for the socket to unscrew the nut (see accompanying photo). As an alternative, a peg spanner can be fabricated from a short length of thick-walled conduit.

4 When the filter body has been removed, the two primary drive pinions can be withdrawn from the splined end of the

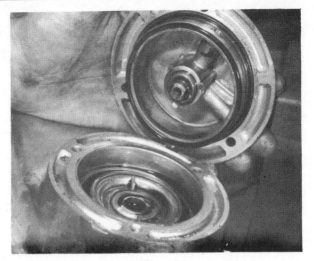
13.1 Outer cover of filter unit is retained by three screws

13.1a Remove crankcase cover for access to primary transmission

13.2 Screw retaining filter cover is recessed in centre

13.3 Body will lift off when sleeve nut is removed

13.3a Welding rod across slots ensures socket spanner is tight fit

13.4 Primary drive pinions have splined centres

14.1a ... and special retaining plate (CB175/CD175 models)

crankshaft. Each pinion is marked with a centre punch dot, to ensure they are replaced as an identical pair with the teeth completely in phase.

14 Dismantling the engine and gearbox - removing the clutch

1   Commence operations by removing the four bolts that pass through the clutch pressure plate. The CB175 and CD175 models have an additional clutch spring retaining plate beneath the bolts that should be lifted off.

2   Withdraw the pressure plate and springs, then lift out the individual clutch plates, five plain and five inserted, spaced alternately.

3   Lift out the clutch pushrod 'mushroom' that presses on the inside of the pressure plate when the clutch is lifted. This will expose the circlip that retains the clutch inner drum in position. Detach the circlip and lift off the inner drum.

4   The clutch outer drum and integral driven pinion can now be drawn off the gearbox mainshaft. The rod that operates the oil pump and the eccentric is attached to the rear of the clutch outer drum and it is necessary to slacken and remove the two bolts that retain the oil pump to the crankcase after bending back the tab washers, so that the clutch outer drum and oil pump can be lifted away in unison. When both components are clear of the engine, the pump rod can be disengaged from the slot in the oil pump plunger.

14.2   Clutch assembly comprises ten plates, five plain, five inserted

14.1 Pressure plate and clutch springs are secured by four bolts ...

14.3 Clutch 'mushroom' locates below pressure plate

14.3a Clutch inner drum is secured by a circlip

15 Dismantling the engine and gearbox - removing the kickstarter and gear change mechanism

1 Remove the kickstarter return spring.
2 Detach the circlip from the left hand end of the gear change lever shaft and draw the shaft away from the right hand side of the crankcase. It will be necessary to depress the spring loaded arm that engages with the end of the gear selector drum during this operation, so that the complete assembly can be drawn clear.
3 Remove the stopper arms that engage with the stops and cam of the gear selector drum. They are retained by a nut and washer and are under spring pressure.

14.3b Remove circlip and lift off drum

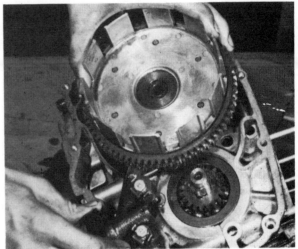

14.4 Clutch outer drum will then lift off mainshaft with oil pump

15.1 Remove kickstarter return spring

15.2 Disengage arm from gear selector drum when withdrawing gear change shaft

15.3 Stopper arms engage with stops and cam of selector drum ...

further examination.

4 To remove the gearbox selector arms, it is necessary to withdraw the gear selector drum. Commence by withdrawing the spring clips from each selector arm so that the pin that engages with the selector drum tracks can be removed with a pair of fine nosed pliers. Some models use hexagon headed pins as an alternative, which thread into the selector arms.

5 Before the selector drum can be removed, it is necessary to first detach the neutral contact which is held to the end of the drum by a crosshead screw, and then remove the bearing retaining plate on the right hand end. On the CB175 models fitted with a five speed gearbox, removal of the guide pins from the three selector arm is made easier if the gear selector drum is partially removed from its housing.

6 When the gear selector drum is withdrawn completely, the selector forks will be released. Take note of the way in which they were assembled originally to aid subsequent reassembly.

7 Remove the bearing retainers from their housings. Those used for the crankshaft main bearings have the greatest length.

15.3a ... remove retaining nut to free stopper arms and spring

16.1 When separating crankcases, note bolt hidden within drain plug orifice

16 Separating the crankcases

1 Invert the engine unit and remove the nine 8 mm bolts and nine 6 mm bolts that hold both crankcases together. Note that one bolt is located within the orifice normally sealed by the crankcase drain plug.

2 The crankcases can now be separated in the inverted position, leaving the upper crankcase together with the various engine and gearbox components resting on the cylinder holding down studs. If the crankcases prove difficult to separate, check that all eighteen bolts have been removed and tap the castings with a rawhide mallet. NEVER use a screwdriver or any other pointed instrument to break the sealed joint if oil leaks after reassembly are to be avoided.

3 Lift out the kickstarter shaft complete, the gearbox mainshaft and the layshaft complete with their respective gear clusters and the complete crankshaft assembly. Place these parts aside for

16.2 Separate with crankcases in the inverted position

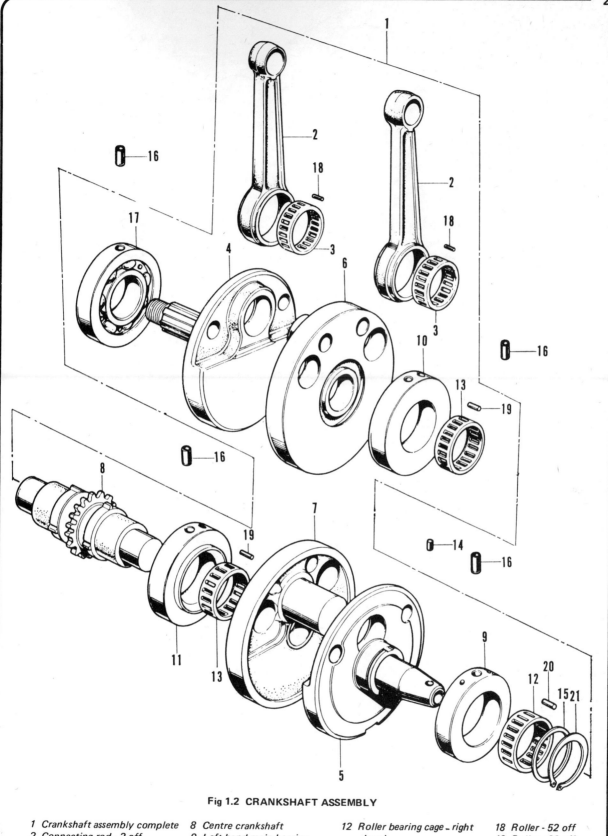

Fig 1.2 CRANKSHAFT ASSEMBLY

1 Crankshaft assembly complete
2 Connecting rod - 2 off
3 Big end roller cage - 2 off
4 Crankshaft - right hand
5 Crankshaft - left hand
6 Centre flywheel - right hand
7 Centre flywheel - left hand
8 Centre crankshaft
9 Left hand main bearing outer race
10 Right hand main bearing outer race
11 Centre bearing race - left hand
12 Roller bearing cage - right hand
13 Roller bearing cage - 2 off
14 Dowel pin
15 Washer
16 Dowel pin - 4 off
17 Ball bearing
18 Roller - 52 off
19 Roller - 30 off
20 Roller - 20 off
21 Circlip

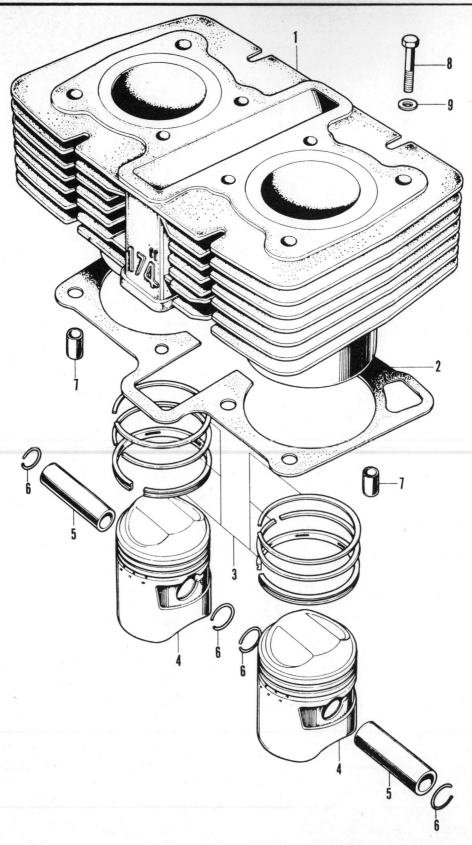

Fig 1.3 CYLINDER BARREL AND PISTONS

1 Cylinder barrel	4 Piston - 2 off	6 Circlip - 4 off	8 Bolt
2 Cylinder base gasket	5 Gudgeon pin - 2 off	7 Dowel pin - 2 off	9 Washer
3 Piston ring set - 2 off			

16.3 Lift out kickstarter shaft assembly complete, followed by ...

16.3a ... gearbox mainshaft gear cluster and ...

16.3b ... gearbox layshaft gear cluster

16.3c Crankshaft assembly lifts out next

16.4 Make note of selector arm locations before removing spring clips

16.4a Use thin nosed pliers to extract pins

16.5 Detach neutral contact lead wire ...

16.5a ... then contact assembly from end of selector drum

16.6 Selector forks are released when drum is withdrawn

17 Examination and renovation - general

1   Before examining the parts of the dismantled engine for wear, it is essential that they should first be cleaned thoroughly. Use a petrol/paraffin mix to remove all traces of old oil and sludge that may have accumulated within the engine.

2   Examine the various castings for cracks or other signs of damage, especially the crankcase castings. If a crack is discovered, it will require professional repair, or replacement.

3   Examine carefully each part to determine the extent of wear, checking with the tolerance figures listed in the Specifications section of this Chapter. If there is any question of doubt, play safe and renew. Notes included in the following text will indicate what type of wear can be expected and whether the part concerned can be reclaimed.

4   Use a clean, lint-free rag for cleaning and drying the various components. This will obviate the risk of small particles obstructing the internal oilways, causing the lubrication system to fail.

5   Above all, work in clean, well-lit surroundings so that faults do not pass undetected. Failure to detect a fault or signs of advanced wear may necessitate a further complete strip down at a later date, due to the premature failure of the part concerned.

18 Big ends and main bearings - examination and renovation

1   The crankshaft assembly can be regarded as two separate sets of flywheels and connecting rods, pressed together by means of a central coupling which carries the camshaft chain drive sprocket. It is not possible to separate the crankshaft assembly without access to the appropriate press equipment or to re-align the dismantled assembly to a sufficiently high standard of accuracy by amateur means. In consequence, it is imperative that the complete flywheel is entrusted to a Honda agent for repair, who will have either the necessary repair facilities or a service-exchange replacement.

2   Failure of the big end bearings is invariably accompanied by a whirring noise from within the crankcase which progressively gets worse. Some vibration will also be experienced. There should be no vertical play whatsoever in either of the connecting rods after the old oil has been washed out of the bearings. If even a small amount of play is evident, the bearing concerned is due for replacement. Do not run the machine with worn big end bearings, otherwise there is risk of causing extensive damage by the breakage of a connecting rod or the crankshaft.

3   Do not confuse big end wear with side play, a certain amount of which is acceptable in the big end bearing assembly. It is permissible to move the small end of each connecting rod sideways not more than 3 mm (0.12 inches) if the amount of sideplay is within acceptable limits.

4   The crankshaft main bearings are of the journal ball type. If wear is evident in the form of play or if the bearings feel rough as they are rotated, they should be replaced. This again is a specialist repair job, necessitating the services of a Honda agent. The crankshaft assembly must be separated to gain access to the two innermost bearings and re-aligned with great accuracy after these bearings have been replaced. It is essential that the correct replacement bearings are fitted and not pattern parts. The bearings are grooved to correspond with the bearing retainers and have a drilling to locate with a dowel pin in the bearing housing.

5   Failure of the main bearings is usually characterised by an audible rumble from the bottom end of the engine, accompanied by vibration. The vibration will be especially noticeable through the footrests.

19 Cylinder block - examination and renovation

1   The usual indications of badly worn cylinders and pistons are excessive oil consumption accompanied by blue smoke from the

exhausts and piston slap, a metallic rattle that occurs when there is little or no load on the engine. If the top of each cylinder bore is examined carefully, it will be found there is a ridge on the thrust side, denoting the limit of travel of the uppermost piston ring. The depth of this ridge will vary according to the amount of wear that has taken place.

2 Measure the bore diameter just below the ridge, using an internal micrometer. Compare this reading with the diameter close to the bottom of the cylinder bore, which has not been subjected to wear. If the difference in readings exceeds 0.005 inch, it is necessary to have the cylinder block rebored and to fit oversize pistons and rings.

3 If an internal micrometer is not available, the amount of wear can be checked by inserting each piston in turn (without rings) into the bore with which it was previously associated. If it is possible to insert a 0.004 inch feeler gauge between the piston and the cylinder wall on the thrust side, remedial action must be taken.

4 Check the surface of each cylinder bore for score marks or other damage that may have resulted from an earlier engine seizure or displacement of a gudgeon pin and/or circlip. A rebore will be necessary to remove any deep indentations, irrespective of the amount of bore wear, otherwise a compression leak will occur.

5 Check that the external cooling fins are not clogged with oil or road dirt, otherwise the engine will overheat. The fins can be cleaned with a wire brush, provided care is taken to ensure the fins are not broken or badly scratched.

20 Pistons and piston rings - examination and renovation

1 If a rebore is necessary, the existing pistons and rings can be disregarded as they will be replaced with their oversize equivalents as a matter of course.

2 Remove all traces of carbon from each piston crown, using a soft scraper to ensure the surface is not marked. Finish off by polishing each crown with metal polish, to give a smooth mirror-like surface to which carbon will not adhere so readily in the future. Never use emery cloth, the particles of which will embed in the soft aluminium alloy.

3 Piston wear usually occurs at the skirt or lower end of the pistons and takes the form of vertical streaks or score marks on the thrust side. There may also be some variation in the thickness of the skirt.

4 The piston ring grooves may become enlarged in use, allowing the piston rings to have greater side float. If the clearance exceeds 0.004 inch for the two compression rings or 0.005 inch for the oil control ring, the pistons are due for replacement. It is unusual however for this form of wear to occur on its own.

5 Piston ring wear is measured by inserting the piston rings in their respective bores, one at a time, using the skirt of the piston to locate them approximately one inch from the base of the inverted cylinder block. Make sure the ring rests square with the bore before measuring the end gap with a feeler gauge. If the gap exceeds 0.014 inch in the case of the two compression rings, or 0.012 inch in the case of the oil control ring, they must be replaced, assuming the cylinder is not in need of a rebore.

21 Cylinder heads - dismantling, examination and renovation of valves, valve seats and valve guides

1 The cylinder head has been removed as a complete casting and still contains the overhead camshaft, the rocker gear and both sets of valves. Further dismantling is necessary to remove these components, for examination and whatever renovation is necessary.

2 Commence by removing the polished alloy cover on the left hand side of the cylinder head. This is retained by two crosshead screws. Remove the two crosshead screws that retain the contact breaker baseplate, and remove the baseplate, complete with the contact breaker points and the connecting wire.

3 Remove the bolt and washer that retains the contact breaker cam and the automatic advance assembly in position, and draw this assembly from the end of the camshaft. Note that a pin in the end of the camshaft ensures the contact breaker cam can be replaced in a set position only. Remove also the casting, retained by four crosshead screws.

4 Remove both spark plugs and the four valve clearance inspection covers. The latter thread into the cylinder head casting and have O ring seals.

5 If it has not already been detached, remove the cover from the right hand side of the cylinder head. This is usually retained by four crosshead screws, but the number may vary, according to the model.

6 Withdraw the four rocker arm shafts, using a pair of thin nosed pliers, if necessary. If a valve is open, the valve clearance adjuster of the rocker arm concerned should be slackened off to release the spring pressure. When the rocker arm shafts have been withdrawn, the rocker arms can be lifted out. Mark them to ensure replacement in the same order.

7 Before the camshaft can be moved across to the right hand side of the cylinder head casting and lifted out, it is necessary to pull the tachometer drive pinion from the left hand end of the camshaft and the dowel that locates it. This will give sufficient clearance for the camshaft, complete with sprocket, to be lifted clear.

8 A valve spring compressor is necessary to remove the valve springs and valves. When the springs are compressed, the split collets can be lifted out from the top cap, enabling the valve to be released when the compressor is unscrewed. Place the components associated with each valve in separate boxes, to ensure they are assembled together again. Make a note of whether the valves came from the left hand or the right hand cylinder head; it is not possible to interchange the inlet and the exhaust valves because the inlet valves have larger diameter heads.

9 Remove all traces of carbon from the cylinder heads and the valve ports, taking care not to scratch the valve seats. Use a soft scraper, otherwise scratch marks may cause hot spots and leakages. Finish by polishing both combustion chambers with metal polish so that carbon will not adhere so easily in the future. Do NOT use emery cloth.

10 Check that the valve guides are free from carbon and burnt oil which may otherwise cause the valves to stick. Make sure the threads of the spark plug holes are clean too.

11 The cylinder head fins must be clean and not clogged with oil or road dirt. Use a wire brush if necessary, taking care not to damage or scratch the fins.

12 After cleaning the valves to remove all traces of carbon, examine the heads for pitting and burning at the ground seating. Examine the condition of the valve seats in the cylinder heads. The exhaust valves and their seats will most likely require the most attention because they run at a higher temperature than the inlet valves. If the pitting is slight, the marks can be removed by grinding the valves and their seats together, using fine grinding compound.

13 Valve grinding is a simple task, carried out as follows: Smear a trace of fine valve grinding compound (carborundum paste) on the seat face and apply a small valve suction grinding tool to the head of the valve. With a semi-rotary motion, grind in the valve head to its seat, using a backward and forward action. It is advisable to lift the valve occasionally to distribute the grinding compound evenly. Repeat this operation until an unbroken ring of light grey matt finish is obtained on both the valve and the seat, completely free from pit marks. This denotes the grinding operation is complete. Before passing on to the next valve, make quite sure that all traces of the grinding compound have been removed from both the valve and its seat and that none has entered the valve guide. If this precaution is not observed, rapid wear will take place, due to the highly abrasive nature of the carborundum paste.

14 Where deeper pit marks are encountered, it will be necessary to use a valve refacing machine and a valve seat cutter, set to an angle of 45°. Never resort to excessive grinding because this will

only pocket the valve and lead to reduced engine efficiency. If there is any doubt about the condition of a valve, fit a new replacement.

15 Examine the condition of the valve collets and the portion of the valve stem on which they seat. If there are any signs of damage, new replacements must be fitted. Check also that the valve caps are free from cracks. If the collets work loose or if a valve cap opens up whilst the engine is running, a valve will drop in and cause extensive damage.

16 Measure the valve stems for wear, making reference to the tolerance values given in the Specifications section of this Chapter. Check the valve guides. If wear is evident, it will be necessary to warm the cylinder head and drive the old guides out from inside the cylinder head, using a two diameter drift, the initial lead of which is the same diameter as the valve stem. Drive the replacement guide into position with the same drift, whilst the cylinder head is still warm. The valve stem clearance should not exceed 0.003 inch inlet or 0.004 inch exhaust. Note that when new valve guides are fitted, it will be necessary to regrind or recut the valve seats.

17 Check the free length of each valve spring against the list of tolerances in the Specifications section of this Chapter. If the springs are reduced in free length or if there is any doubt about their condition, they should be replaced.

21.3 Remove contact breaker housing to release left hand end of camshaft

21.5   Other end of camshaft is retained by tachometer drive housing

21.6 Rocker arm shafts will pull out of cylinder head casting

21.7 Move camshaft to right hand side before lifting out

22 Camshaft and camshaft chain sprocket - examination

1   Examine the camshaft chain sprocket for worn, broken or chipped teeth, an unusual occurrence that can be attributed to the presence of foreign bodies or particles from some other broken engine component. The sprocket is integral with the camshaft and the complete assembly must be replaced if signs of wear or damage are evident.

2   The cams should have a smooth surface and be entirely free from scuff marks or indentations. It is unlikely that severe wear will be encountered during the normal service life of the machine unless the lubrication system has failed, causing the case hardened surface to wear through.

3   Make sure the timing mark is clearly visible on the camshaft chain sprocket. It will be necessary to refer to this mark when the engine is retimed.

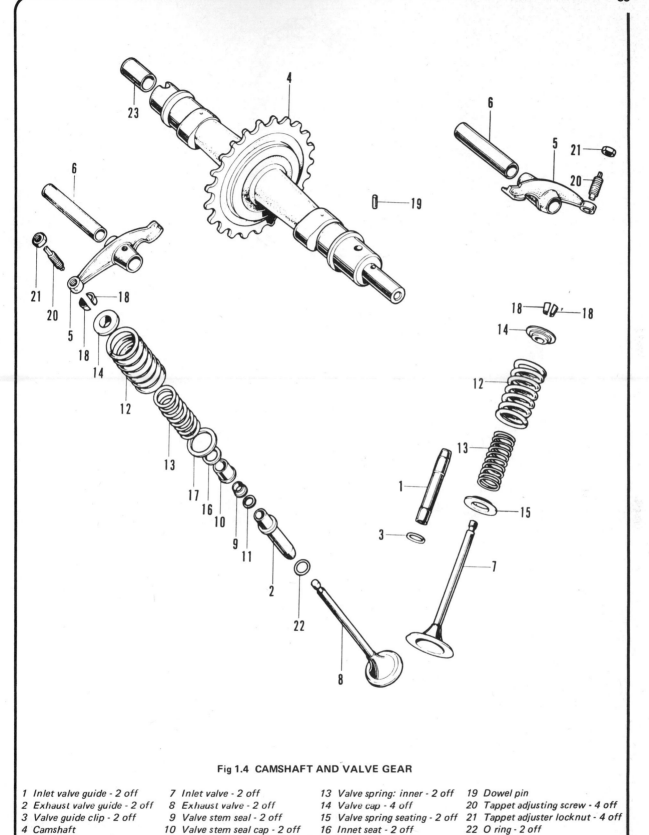

Fig 1.4 CAMSHAFT AND VALVE GEAR

1 Inlet valve guide - 2 off
2 Exhaust valve guide - 2 off
3 Valve guide clip - 2 off
4 Camshaft
5 Rocker arm - 4 off
6 Rocker shaft - 4 off

7 Inlet valve - 2 off
8 Exhaust valve - 2 off
9 Valve stem seal - 2 off
10 Valve stem seal cap - 2 off
11 Valve stem seal rubber - 2 off
12 Valve spring: outer - 2 off

13 Valve spring: inner - 2 off
14 Valve cap - 4 off
15 Valve spring seating - 2 off
16 Innet seat - 2 off
17 Outer seat - 2 off
18 Split collets - 8 off

19 Dowel pin
20 Tappet adjusting screw - 4 off
21 Tappet adjuster locknut - 4 off
22 O ring - 2 off
23 Dowel pin

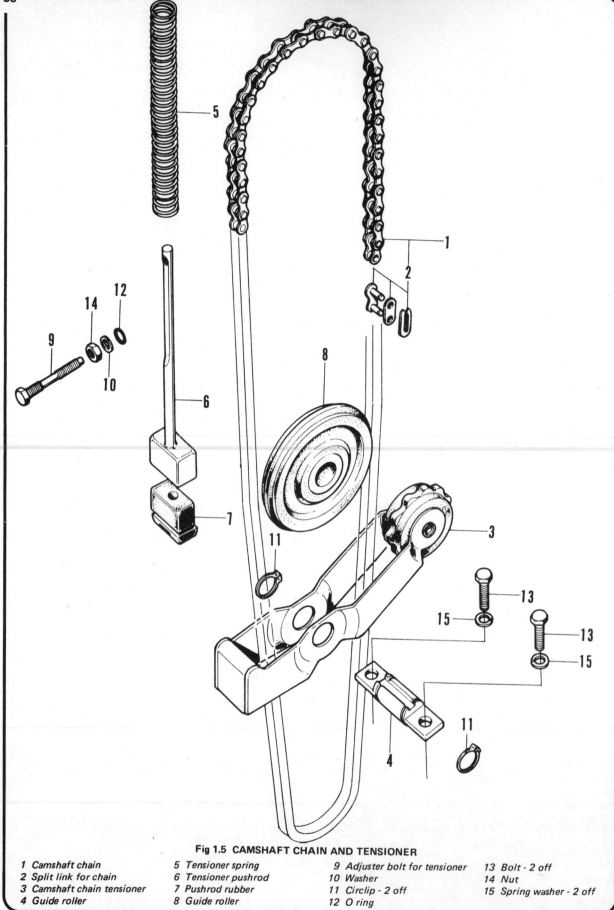

Fig 1.5 CAMSHAFT CHAIN AND TENSIONER

1 Camshaft chain	5 Tensioner spring	9 Adjuster bolt for tensioner	13 Bolt - 2 off
2 Split link for chain	6 Tensioner pushrod	10 Washer	14 Nut
3 Camshaft chain tensioner	7 Pushrod rubber	11 Circlip - 2 off	15 Spring washer - 2 off
4 Guide roller	8 Guide roller	12 O ring	

23 Rocker arms and rocker shafts - examination

1 It is unlikely that excessive wear will occur in either the rocker arms or the rocker shafts unless the flow of oil has been impeded or the machine has covered a very large mileage. A clicking noise from the rocker area is the usual symptom of wear in the rocker gear, which should not be confused with a somewhat similar noise caused by excessive valve clearances.

2 If any shake is present and the rocker arm is loose on its shaft, a new rocker arm and/or shaft should be fitted.

3 Check the tip of each rocker arm at the point where the arm makes contact with the cam. If signs of cracking, scuffing or break through in the case hardened surface are evident, fit a new replacement.

4 Check also the thread of the tappet adjusting screw, the thread of the rocker arm into which it fits and the thread of the locknut. The hardened end of the tappet adjuster must also be in good condition.

24 Camshaft chain, chain tensioner and lower camshaft chain sprocket - examination

1 Each of these components is lubricated by the return flow of oil from the camshaft and rocker gear and it is unlikely that excessive wear will occur unless there is a lubrication failure or parts of some broken engine component become entangled. Wear or damage to the sprocket teeth will immediately be obvious; if the sprocket is damaged or badly worn the chain must be replaced. The chain tensioner roller will wear to a smooth profile and should be replaced if the tooth-like indentations are no longer evident. The tensioner arm bolts direct to the upper crankcase, in between the two cylinder barrels. The roller is retained on the pin around which it revolves, by two circlips.

2 A worn camshaft drive chain will cause a distinctive rattle that will not disappear, even when the tensioner is re-adjusted. Some indication of the amount of wear that has taken place is given if the chain is held at both ends and twisted sideways. A badly worn chain will bend into a pronounced arc. If there is any doubt about the condition of the chain, it should be renewed without question. If a chain breakage occurs, serious engine damage may occur.

3 Check that the spring link joining the chain ends is in good condition. The closed end of the spring should always face the direction of travel of the chain, so that it is less likely to be displaced.

4 Examine the rubber pad on the end of the chain tensioner bar. If it is worn or damaged, it should be replaced. The pad is a push fit in the holder.

25 Gearbox components - examination

1 Give the gearbox components a close visual examination for signs of wear or damage such as chipped or broken teeth, worn dogs or worn splines and bent selector arms. If the machine has shown a tendency to jump out of gear, look especially for worn dogs on the back of the gear pinions or wear in the selector tracks of the gear selector drum. In the former case, wear will be evident in the form of rounded corners or even a wedge-shaped profile in an extreme case. The corners of the selector drum tracks will wear first; all such wear is characterised by the brightly polished surface.

2 The selector arms usually wear across the fork that engages with a gear pinion, causing a certain amount of sloppiness in the gear change movement. A bent selector will immediately be obvious, especially if overheating has blued the surface.

3 All gearbox components that prove faulty will have to be replaced. There is no satisfactory method of reclaiming them.

26 Clutch - examination and renovation

1 Check the condition of the clutch drive, to ensure none of the teeth are chipped, broken or badly worn.

2 Give the plain and the inserted plates a wash with a petrol/paraffin mix and check that they are not buckled or distorted. Remove all traces of clutch insert debris, otherwise a gradual build-up will occur and affect clutch action.

3 Visual inspection will show whether the tongues of the clutch plates have become burred and whether corresponding indentations have formed in the slots with which they engage. Burrs should be removed with a file, which can also be used to dress the slots square once again, provided the depth of the indentations is not too great.

4 Check the thickness of the friction linings in the inserted plates. The standard thickness is 3 mm. When the thickness is reduced to 2.9 mm, the inserted plates must be replaced. Always renew them as a complete set, irrespective of whether some may not have reached the serviceable limit. Worn linings promote clutch slip.

5 Check the free length of the clutch springs against the Specifications section of this Chapter. Do not stretch the springs if they have compressed. They must be replaced as a complete set when the serviceable limit has been reached.

6 Check the clutch pushrod for straightness, if necessary by rolling it on a sheet of glass. Heavy action is often caused by a bent rod, which may pick up in its housing. Check the action of the clutch actuating mechanism that is located on the inside of the left hand crankcase cover which contains also the generator stator coil assembly. The mechanism operates on the quick thread principle and should give no trouble if greased regularly.

27 Reassembling the cylinder heads

1 Replace the four valves, reversing the dismantling procedure described in Section 21 of this Chapter. Make sure the valve collets are seated correctly; a light tap on the end of each valve stem, after assembly, is a good check. Do not omit to oil the valve stems before the valves are inserted in the guides, to obviate the risk of running dry until the oil has circulated throughout the engine.

2 Oil the rocker shafts and the ends of the rocker arms where they bear on the camshaft. Insert or turn the camshaft until the O timing mark is uppermost, in the twelve o'clock position. This will aid the timing of the engine during reassembly.

3 Use new gaskets between the right and left hand covers that retain the camshaft and rocker shafts, without gasket cement. There is an oil seal within the left hand cover to prevent oil from reaching the contact breaker points. This should be renewed, even if it has not previously shown signs of leakage.

28 Engine and gearbox reassembly - general

1 Before reassembly is commenced, the various engine and gearbox components should be cleaned thoroughly and placed close to the working area.

2 Make sure all traces of old gaskets have been removed and that the mating surfaces are clean and undamaged. One of the best ways in which to remove old gasket cement is to apply a rag soaked in methylated spirits. This acts as a solvent and will ensure the cement is moved without resort to scraping and the consequent risk of damage.

3 Gather together all the necessary tools and have available an oil can filled with clean engine oil. Make sure all the new gaskets, oil seals and replacement parts are available; there is nothing more frustrating than having to stop in the middle of a reassembly

sequence because a vital gasket or part has been overlooked. If it is necessary to make a gasket, extreme care should be taken to ensure the profile is identical to that of the original. It is not sufficient to cut around the edges. For example, the right hand crankcase cover has two oil passageways within the periphery and if the gasket does not encircle them, there will be a complete lack of oil pressure followed by an engine seizure. Use genuine Honda gaskets whenever possible, which will obviate this problem.

4   Make sure the reassembly area is clean and well lit, with adequate working space. Refer to the torque and clearance settings wherever they are given. Many of the smaller bolts are easily sheared if overtightened. Always use the correct size screwdriver bit for the crosshead screws and NEVER an ordinary screwdriver or punch. Remember that if the heads are badly damaged during reassembly, the screws may prove almost impossible to undo on the next occasion.

29 Engine and gearbox reassembly - rebuilding the gearbox

1   Invert the upper crankcase and place it on the workbench. Commence reassembly by re-inserting the gear selector drum, after positioning the gear selector arms in their correct positions, over the drum as it is slid into position. Replace the drum retaining plate, held by two countersunk screws.

2   Insert the guide pins in each selector arm and check that they engage with each track correctly. Note that in the case of the CB175 five-speed models, where spring clips are used to retain the guide pins, the direction in which the pins face must be correct. If the centre clip is replaced from the wrong direction, it will foul a gear pinion. Refer to the accompanying illustration for the correct layout.

3   Replace the layshaft gear cluster after ensuring the bearing retainers have been correctly relocated. Check also that the selector arm engages correctly with the sliding gear pinion.

4   Replace the mainshaft gear cluster and check that the selector arm(s) engage correctly with the sliding pinion(s).

5   Position the kickstarter shaft assembly immediately to the rear of the layshaft and check that the pinion engages correctly as the shaft is rotated.

29.1 Insert selector drum after positioning selector arms in correct order

29.2 Insert selector pins to engage with tracks on drum

29.2a Spring clips must be positioned as shown or they may foul gear pinions

29.3 Replace gearbox layshaft gear cluster and engage with selector arms

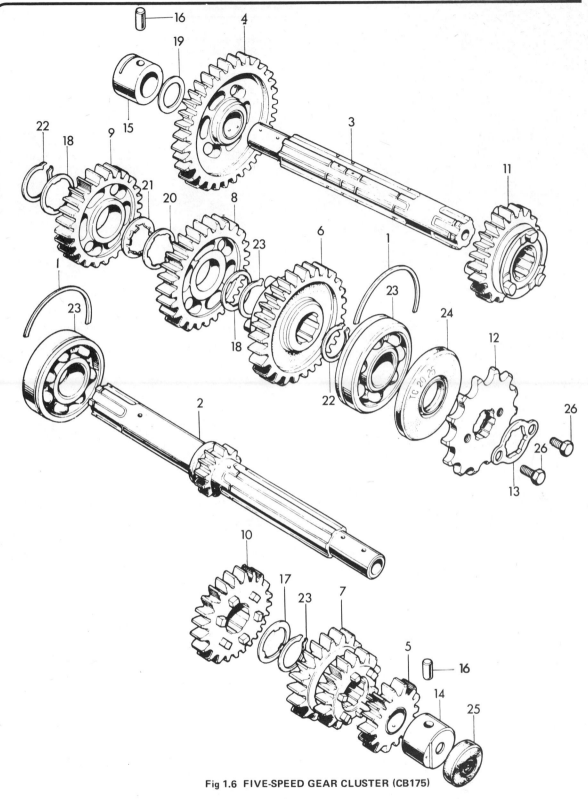

Fig 1.6 FIVE-SPEED GEAR CLUSTER (CB175)

1 Bearing retainer - 2 off
2 Mainshaft (13 teeth pinion)
3 Layshaft
4 Layshaft first gear (36 teeth)
5 Mainshaft second gear (17 teeth)
6 Layshaft second gear (32 teeth)
7 Mainshaft sliding gear (20 and 23 teeth)
8 Layshaft third gear (29 teeth)
9 Layshaft fourth gear (27 teeth)

10 Mainshaft fifth gear (25 teeth)
11 Layshaft fifth gear (25 teeth)
12 Final drive sprocket (number of teeth according to model)
13 Sprocket locking plate
14 Bearing bush - mainshaft
15 Bearing bush - layshaft
16 Guide pin for selector fork - 2 off
17 Thrust washer - 20 mm

18 Thrust washer - 20 mm - 2 off
19 Thrust washer - 16 mm
20 Thrust washer - 20 mm
21 Lockwasher - 20 mm
22 Circlip - 2 off
23 Ball bearing - 2 off
24 Oil seal
25 Oil seal
26 Bolt - 2 off

29.4 Replace gearbox mainshaft gear cluster in similar fashion

29.5 Kickstarter shaft assembly is positioned next

30 Engine and gearbox reassembly - replacing the crankshaft and joining the crankcases

1   Replace the crankshaft bearing retainers and lower the crankshaft assembly into position, after first aligning the bearings so that the drillings in the outer races line up with the dowel pins in the bearing housings. There is a line scribed on the outer race of each main bearing which lines up with the edge of the bearing housing (viewed from the rear) when the drilling and dowel pin are in line. This will aid assembly. Check that the connecting rods are fed through the crankcase mouths.

2   It may be necessary to give each end of the crankshaft a light tap with a mallet to make sure the bearings seat correctly. This also applies to the gearbox shafts and bearings. If any bearing is out of place, the crankcases will not join.

3   Thread the camshaft drive chain over the lower sprocket and temporarily anchor the ends.

4   Give the mating surface of the lower crankcase a smearing of gasket cement and lower it into position on the inverted upper crankcase. Check again that the bearings are located correctly and that the upper and lower crankcases fit together, without applying pressure.

5   Replace the nine 8 mm bolts and the nine 6 mm bolts that hold both crankcases together. Note that the 8 mm bolt immediately to the rear of the drain plug orifice has the starter cable clamp attached. Tighten the bolts carefully to a torque setting of 11.5 to 12.2 lb f ft (8 mm bolts) and 5.8 to 6.5 lb f ft (6 mm bolts). One 6 mm bolt is located within the drain plug orifice.

30.1 Locate crankshaft bearing retainers ...

30.1a Scribe line on bearing aids correct location

30.3 Do not omit to loop camshaft chain around lower sprocket

30.3a Anchor ends with length of welding rod

30.4 Check bearings have registered correctly before fitting lower crankcase

30.5 Do not omit 8 mm bolt within drain plug orifice ...

30.5a ... then replace and tighten drain plug

31 Engine and gearbox reassembly - replacing the gear change mechanism

1   Commence by replacing the neutral contact in the end of the gear selector drum. The rotor takes the form of an insulator with a metal contact and it is pegged so that it can be attached to the end of the drum in one set position only. It is retained by a central crosshead screw.

2   The plate with which contact is made is attached to the outer face of the crankcase by a crosshead screw.

3   Replace selector drum retainer. Reassemble the stopper arms and springs that bear on the stop pins and cam at the end of the gear selector drum. This is a somewhat tricky operation, necessitating reference to the accompanying illustration as a check that the parts are positioned in the correct order.

4   Fit a new oil seal for the gear change shaft on the left hand side of the engine and insert the gear change shaft from the right. Engage the spring tensioned gear change arm with the stop pins on the end of the gear selector drum and check that the ends of the return spring are either side of the return spring pin. Reverting to the left hand side again, replace the washer in front of the oil seal and the circlip that retains the shaft in position.

5   It is opportune to fit the final drive sprocket at the same time if the chain has been separated. The splined centre of the sprocket fits over the end of the gearbox layshaft, which has matching splines, and is retained by a locking plate and two 6 mm bolts which must be tight.

32 Engine and gearbox reassembly - replacing the clutch and primary drive

1   Slide the first of the paired primary drive pinions on the right hand end of the crankshaft.

2   Lower the clutch outer drum into position on the gearbox mainshaft splines so that the integral driven gear meshes with the primary drive pinion. It will be necessary to attach the oil pump at the same time, reconnected with the pump operating arm behind the clutch. The pump is secured by two bolts and two washers. Then replace the second of the primary drive pinions, noting that the centre punch mark on the face must line up with that of the pinion already on the crankshaft. This will ensure the sprockets match up correctly with the staggered teeth formation of the clutch drum driven pinion.

3   Replace the clutch inner drum and the circlip that retains it in position. The clutch plates can now be refitted, commencing with the plain dished plate. The clutch has a total of ten plates, five plain and five inserted, which are fitted in alternate order.

4   Before the pressure plate and clutch springs are fitted, the clutch operating 'mushroom' must be inserted into the end of the hollow mainshaft. Make sure the shaft is oiled.

5   Replace the pressure plate, clutch springs and the retaining plate (late models only). Replace also the 6 mm bolts and tighten them fully.

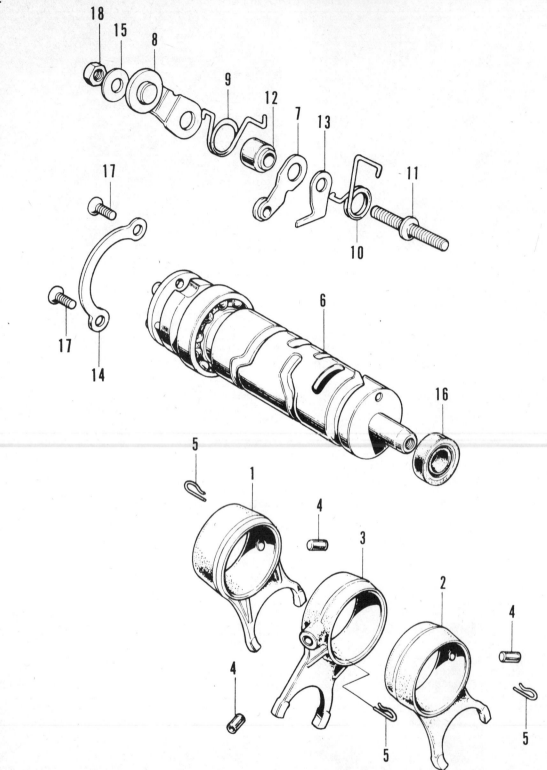

Fig 1.7 GEAR CHANGE MECHANISM (CB175)

1 Gear selector fork, right hand
2 Gear selector fork, left hand
3 Gear selector fork, centre
4 Guide pin for gear selector fork - 3 off
5 Clip for guide pin - 3 off
6 Gear selector drum
7 Neutral stopper arm

8 Gear change drum stopper arm
9 Spring for gear change drum stopper
10 Spring for neutral stopper
11 Pin for gear change drum stopper
12 Collar for gear change drum stopper
13 Stopper arm plate
14 Bearing retainer

15 Washer for gear change drum stopper
16 Oil seal
17 Countersunk screw for bearing retainer - 2
     off
18 Nut

31.2 Replace neutral contact in end of selector drum

31.3 Selector drum retainer is added next, followed by ...

31.3a ... stopper arm spring and stopper plate, then ...

31.3b ... drum stopper, spring and retaining nut and washer

31.4 Fit new oil seal to gear change shaft housing

31.4a Replace gear change shaft from right hand side and engage with selector drum

31.4b Fit washer and circlip to left hand end of shaft

31.5 Place final drive sprocket on layshaft splines, then ...

31.5a ... fit locking plate as retainer

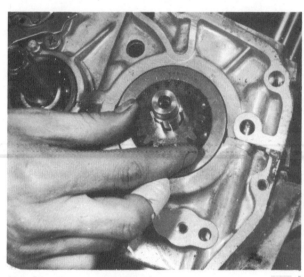

32.1 Slide first primary drive pinion on crankshaft

32.2 Lower clutch outer drum in unison with oil pump

32.2a Pinion marks must align to ensure correct mesh ...

32.2b ... when second pinion is fitted

32.3 Replace inner drum ...

32.3a ... secure with circlip ...

32.3b ... and replace the clutch plates

32.4 Do not omit clutch 'mushroom' before ...

32.4a ... replacing pressure plate and tightening bolts fully

33 Engine and gearbox reassembly - replacing the oil filter and right hand cover

1 The outer body of the centrifugal oil filter fits over the splined end of the crankshaft, on the right hand side immediately in front of the primary drive pinions. It is held in position by a sleeve nut which can be tightened fully by using either of the methods described in Section 13.3 of this Chapter if the Honda service tool is not available. Lock the nut in place by the tab washer that seats beneath it.

2 Replace the oil filter cap which is retained by a centre crosshead screw. Make sure the centre screw is tight. The cap has an O ring seal which must be in good condition. The cap will fit correctly only if one of the internal vanes locates with the guide in the outer body.

3 Refit the kickstarter return spring and tension it so that the right angled end abuts against the inner surface of the crankcase casting.

4 Replace the right hand cover using a new gasket without any gasket cement on the mating faces. The cover is retained by a total of eleven crosshead screws.

5 Place a new O ring seal in the orifice around the centrifugal oil filter, then replace the oil filter cover which is retained by three crosshead screws. Check that the central pressure release valve moves freely before replacing the cover. It should press inwards.

33.2 Locate vanes with guide in outer body when replacing end cover

33.2a Cover is retained by a central, crosshead screw

33.3 Tension kickstarter return spring as shown

33.5 Note O ring seal for outer cover

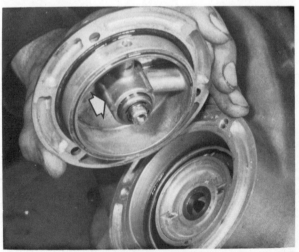

33.5a Check pressure release valve action before replacing outer cover

34 Engine and gearbox reassembly - refitting the starter motor, starter motor drive and clutch

1 Place the starter motor driven sprocket on the end of the crankshaft and then the generator rotor which is a keyed taper fit. Lock the rotor in position with the centre retaining bolt and washer.

2 Refit the starter motor which is retained to the right hand side of the upper crankcase by two crosshead screws. The boss of the motor is a good fit in the extended end of the upper crankcase and it may be necessary to tap the end of the rotor with a mallet in order to drive it fully home.

3 Replace the guide clip that retains the starter motor sprocket in position (one crosshead screw), loop the starter drive chain around the sprocket and engage the smaller starter motor sprocket with the chain before pressing it onto the splined end of the starter motor.

4 If the starter motor chain is tight, it may be necessary to amend the above procedure and fit the starter motor, chain and starter motor sprocket together.

5 Grease and insert the clutch pushrod from the left hand side of the engine, then refit the left hand crankcase cover which is retained by nine crosshead screws. Make sure the green wire is connected to the neutral contact and that the main wiring harness is retained by the clip close to the top of the final drive sprocket so that it is well clear of the chain.

6 A new gasket should be fitted at this joint, and both jointing surfaces given a light smear of gasket cement, to maintain an oil-tight seal.

7 The starter motor is omitted from the UK imported CD175 models.

35 Engine and gearbox reassembly - replacing the pistons and cylinder block

1 Before replacing the pistons, pad the mouth of each crankcase with clean rag in order to prevent any displaced component from accidentally dropping into the crankcase.

2 Fit the pistons in their original order with the larger cutaways (marked IN) on the crown facing towards the REAR of the machine. This is most important, otherwise there is risk of the valves fouling the pistons. The inlet valves have the larger diameter heads.

3 If the gudgeon pins are a tight fit, warm the pistons first to expand the metal. Oil the gudgeon pins, small end bearing surfaces and the piston bosses before fitting.

4 Use new circlips, NEVER the originals, and check that the circlips have located correctly with the groove within each piston boss. A displaced circlip will cause severe engine damage and possibly a seizure. Check the piston rings have been replaced in their correct order. The stepped ring is the middle ring and must be fitted step downwards. As a check, the markings T or R on each ring must face upwards.

5 Position a new cylinder base gasket over the crankcase mouth (no cement), checking to ensure the large cut-outs around the studs are at the rear. Incorrect replacement will cut off the cylinder base oil supply. Place the cylinder block over the holding down studs. Support the block whilst the camshaft chain is threaded through the tensioner and then through the tunnel between the cylinder bores. This task is aided by attaching a length of 1/8 inch diameter welding rod to each end of the chain so that the chain can be drawn up through the tunnel. The chain tensioner is bolted to the top of the crankcase by two bolts and spring washers which must be tight.

6 The cylinder bores have a generous lead in, and it should not be necessary to use ring compressors for the pistons. Slide the cylinder block down the studs and after checking that the piston ring end gaps are not in line, feed the piston rings into each cylinder bore, whilst maintaining a firm downward pressure. When the rings have engaged, remove the rag padding from the crankcase and lower the cylinder block still further until it seats fully on the base gasket. Fit the single retaining bolt at the rear of the block, and tightened after the cylinder head bolts.

7 Take care to anchor the ends of the camshaft drive chain

throughout this operation or the chain will drop into the crankcase. If it does fall into the crankcase, it can usually be hooked out quite successfully with a piece of bent wire. Make sure it re-engages with the lower sprocket.

34.1 Rotor is a keyed taper fit on crankshaft

34.4 Starter motor sprocket has splined fitting

34.5 Grease pushrod prior to insertion

34.5a Cable clip must be replaced to keep wires clear of sprocket

35.1 Pad crankcase with rag before replacing pistons

35.5 Gasket must be positioned with large cutaways at rear, or oil supply is cut off from cylinder head

35.5a Thread camshaft chain through tensioner, then ...

35.5b ... through tunnel between cylinder bores

36 Engine and gearbox reassembly - replacing the cylinder head and re-timing the engine

1 Rotate the crankshaft until the T mark on the face of the generator rotor aligns exactly with the scribe line on the pointer attached to the stator assembly. This may necessitate repositioning the camshaft drive chain on the lower sprocket so that both ends are of equal length. If the ends are held firmly the chain can be temporarily disengaged from the sprocket teeth as it is lowered and re-engaged when raised.

2 Fit a new cylinder head gasket (no cement) over the studs, then position the cylinder head on the studs. Note that the camshaft tensioner rod must be fitted before the cylinder head is placed on the holding down studs and retained in its uppermost position by means of the adjuster and locknut at the front of the cylinder. Do not omit the compression spring that fits over the rod or the 'O' ring over the lock bolt. Push to the fully compressed position and lock.

3 Position the camshaft so that the O inscribed close to the teeth of the sprocket is exactly in the twelve o'clock position and recheck that the T mark on the generator rotor and the scribe line on the pointer coincide exactly.

4 Without turning the engine, feed the camshaft chain through the tunnel in the cylinder head casting, using the two pieces of

wire as previously, then lower the casting until it seats on the head gasket. Detach the wire from each end of the camshaft drive chain and join the chain by means of the spring link with the ends pressed into the sprocket teeth. The closed end of the spring clip must face the direction of travel of the chain ie anti-clockwise when viewed from the left handside. Re-tension the camshaft chain by slackening off the adjuster. The device is self-tensioning. Re-tighten the locknuts.

5   The joining of the camshaft chain is a particularly delicate operation and should not be hurried. If the chain or parts of the spring link assembly are dropped, they will probably fall into the crankcase, necessitating at the very least removal of the cylinder head casting and cylinder block to effect recovery.

6   When the chain has been joined and tensioned, check once again that the timing is correct. It cannot be over-emphasised that an error of only one tooth on the camshaft sprocket will have a profound effect on performance and on the general running of the engine.

7   Lubricate the camshaft and rocker gear with a copious flow of oil, then fit the cylinder head cover, using a new gasket and no gasket cement. The cover is retained by eight acorn nuts, one of which fits over the clip that retains the condenser. Tighten each of the nuts in a diagonal sequence to a torque setting of 11.5 to 14.5 lb f ft. Do not overlook the short bolt that fits

36.1 Align timing marks to register exactly

36.2 Insert tensioner rod and spring; lock in fully compressed position

36.3 T mark on rotor must align accurately with pointer

36.4 Feed camshaft chain through tunnel whilst lowering cylinder head

36.5 Position spring link as shown, viewed from left hand side

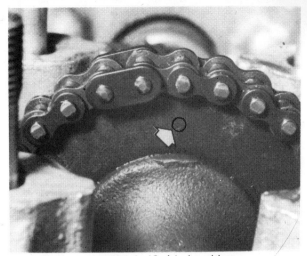

36.6 Check timing mark is in 12 o'clock position

36.7 Fit new cylinder head cover gasket, then ...

36.7a ... cylinder head cover

within the forward mounted head steady lug.

37 Adjusting the valve clearances

1 Whilst the engine is still in the timing position, verify by means of the adjusting holes which cylinder is at top dead centre on the compression stroke. This will be the cylinder where both rocker arms are quite free.

2 Slacken the locknut at the end of each rocker arm and turn the square ended adjuster until a 0.002 inch feeler gauge is a good sliding fit between the end of the rocker arm and the valve stem on which it bears. Tighten the locknut and recheck the gap. Hold the squared end of the adjuster when tightening the locknut to prevent the adjuster from turning and changing the setting. Recheck the setting before passing to the next valve.

3 When both valves have been adjusted, turn the engine through 360º (one complete turn) until the timing marks again coincide and the rocker arms of the other cylinder are quite free. Adjust these valve clearances in a similar manner, not forgetting to recheck.

4 Renew the O ring seals and replace and tighten the four valve inspection caps. Replace also both spark plugs and tighten them down.

37.2 Adjust tappets to recommended clearance of 0.002 inch

38 Engine and gearbox reassembly - replacing the carburettor(s)

1 Fit a new gasket (no cement) to each set of carburettor retaining studs, then the thick heat insulator that precedes each carburettor.

2 Fit a new O ring seal to the flange of each carburettor and place the carburettors over the retaining studs. The carburettor to which the hand operated choke lever is attached should be fitted on the left hand side. Only a single carburettor has to be replaced in the case of the CD175 model.

3 Place a retaining washer and nut on each stud and tighten them down evenly. Do not overtighten or there is danger of bowing the carburettor flange.

4 Couple together the two carburettor chokes by means of the rod that interconnects them. It is secured by a washer and split pin through the end of the operating arm of the right hand instrument.

5 The engine unit is now sufficiently complete for installation in the frame.

38.2 Replace both carburettors using new O ring seals at flange joints

39 Replacing the engine and gearbox unit in the frame

1 Although this can be handled as a single person task, it is advisable to have the assistance of a second person to steady the frame and cycle parts as the engine is lifted in.

2 Lift the complete engine unit into the frame from the right hand side and locate the lower rear engine bolt first. The engine can then be pivotted to permit the upper rear engine bolt to be located, then the front engine plates with their respective bolts (CB175 and CD175 models only) and the plates that form the head steady mounting. Replace the nuts and washers on the ends of these bolts and tighten them fully only after all have been positioned correctly. A torque setting of 3 to 4 lb f ft is recommended for all the engine mounting bolts. Note that the earthing strap fits under the head of the upper rear engine bolt.

3 Refit the final drive chain. Reconnection with the split link is made easier if the ends of the chain are pressed into the rear wheel sprocket, after the chain has been threaded around the final drive sprocket of the gearbox.

4 Remake the electrical connections from the generator wiring harness by means of the various connectors provided. Thread the starter motor cable through the frame and reconnect with the solenoid under the dual seat. This operation is made easier by temporarily removing the left hand air filter. Attach the positive lead to the battery positive terminal and connect the spark plug leads with the spark plugs by means of the push-on plug covers.

5 Reconnect the breather pipe to the rear of the cylinder head cover. Note that the pipe carries a wire clip which acts as a guide for the spark plug leads to keep them away from the hot engine.

6 Replace the air cleaner hoses that are a push-on fit at each carburettor air intake, and retained by wire clips. Replace also the carburettor slides and needles, and tighten the carburettor tops.

7 Re-attach the tachometer cable (if fitted) to the right hand cylinder head cover, retaining it in place with the crosshead screw that clamps the cable. Replace also the chromium plated outer cover secured by a central crosshead screw.

8 Slide the small portion of crankcase containing the clutch cable stop into position, after re-engaging the cable nipple with the clutch actuating mechanism within the left hand outer cover. If necessary, use a screwdriver to raise the operating arm in order to make reconnection easier. Fit the cover over the final drive sprocket that holds the clutch cable stop in position. The cover is

secured by three crosshead screws.

9 Replace the auto-advance mechanism and contact breaker cam in the left hand cylinder head cover, then the contact breaker plate and points assembly. The points are located to the left of the plate. Remake the electrical connections, noting how grommets are provided to keep the wire away from the hotter parts of the engine. Do NOT replace the end cover at this stage. There is a scribe line on the periphery of the base plate which should point to the top.

10 Lower the petrol tank into position and reconnect the underside of both halves of the tank by the rubber tube that joins them. The tube is clamped by a wire clip at each end. Remake also the connections from the petrol tap to the carburettor float chambers.

11 Replace both silencers and exhaust pipes. Attach the silencers loosely after first checking the finned rings are in position. Make the cylinder head joint first, using a new sealing gasket in each case. Fit the split clamps around each pipe, then tighten the finned rings carefully on their respective studs. Finally, tighten the silencer retaining bolts.

12 Refit the footrests and tighten them securely.

13 Locate the kickstarter and gear change lever in their original positions, as denoted by the matching centre punch marks, and tighten them on their splines by means of the clamp bolt.

14 Check the ignition timing by following the procedure described in Chapter 3, Section 7. When the timing is correct, replace the polished alloy end cover of the contact breaker housing (two crosshead screws) and also the circular cover over the rotor of the AC generator (new gasket, three crosshead screws with O ring seals).

15 Check the crankcase drain plug has been replaced and tightened, then refill the engine unit with the correct quantity of oil. The filler is located at the top of the right hand crankcase cover and has an integral dipstick. Rest the plug on top of the filler orifice when taking dipstick readings.

16 Refill with SAE 10W/40 Engine Oil, 1.5 litres CB175 and CD175 models, or 1 litre in the case of the CB125 and CB160 models. Do not overfill.

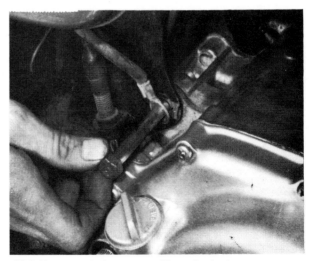

39.2 Upper rear bolt acts as earthing point for battery strap

39.7 Reconnect tachometer drive cable with gearbox drive

39.8 Reconnect clutch cable and locate clutch cable stop

39.9 The auto-advance mechanism precedes the contact breaker assembly ...

39.9a ... which is attached by two screws

39.9b Note location of grommet to seal contact breaker housing

39.9c Also to keep wire off hot cylinder head fins

39.9d Do not omit the all-important connection to the condenser

39.15 Refill engine unit with oil

39.16 Check the ignition timing before replacing the contact breaker cover ···

39.16a ... and the generator cover. Don't forget the gasket!

40 Starting and running the rebuilt engine

1   Open the petrol tap, close the carburettor chokes and start the engine using either the kickstarter or the electric starter. Raise the chokes as soon as the engine will run evenly and keep it running at a low speed for a few moments to permit the oil to circulate through the lubrication system.

2   The engine may show a tendency to smoke initially due to the amount of oil used during assembly of the various components. The excess oil should gradually burn away as the engine settles down.

3   Check the exterior of the machine for oil leaks or blowing gaskets. Make sure each gear engages correctly and that all controls function effectively, particularly the brakes. This is an essential last check before taking the machine on the road.

41 Taking the rebuilt machine on the road

1   Any rebuilt machine will need time to settle down, even if parts have been replaced in their original order. For this reason it is highly advisable to treat the machine gently for the first few miles to ensure oil has circulated throughout the lubrication system and that any new parts fitted have begun to bed down.

2   Even greater care is necessary if the engine has been rebored or if a new crankshaft has been fitted. In the case of a rebore, the engine will have to be run-in again, as if the machine were new. This means greater use of the gearbox and a restraining hand on the throttle until at least 500 miles have been covered. There is no point in keeping to any set speed limit; the main requirement is to keep a light loading on the engine and to gradually work up performance until the 500 mile mark is reached. These recommendations can be lessened to an extent when only a new crankshaft is fitted. Experience is the best guide since it is easy to tell when an engine is running freely.

3   If at any time a lubrication failure is suspected, stop the engine immediately and investigate the cause. If an engine is run without oil, even for a short period, irreparable engine damage is inevitable.

4   When the engine has cooled down completely after the initial run, recheck the various settings, especially the valve clearances. During the run most of the engine components will have settled down into their normal working locations.

42 Fault diagnosis - engine

Symptom	Cause	Remedy
Engine will not start	Defective spark plugs	Remove the plugs and lay on cylinder heads. Check whether spark occurs when ignition is switched on and engine rotated.
	Dirty or closed contact breaker points	Check condition of points and whether gap is correct.
	Faulty or disconnected condenser	Check whether points arc when separated. Replace condenser if evidence of arcing.
Engine runs unevenly	Ignition and/or fuel system fault	Check each system independently, as though engine will not start.
	Blowing cylinder head gasket	Leak should be evident from oil leakage where gas escapes.
	Incorrect ignition timing	Check accuracy and if necessary reset.
Lack of power	Fault in fuel system or incorrect ignition timing	See above.
Heavy oil consumption	Cylinder barrels in need of rebore	Check for bore wear, rebore and fit over-size pistons if required.
	Damaged oil seals	Check engine for oil leaks.
Excessive mechanical noise	**Worn cylinder barrels (piston slap)**	Rebore and fit oversize pistons.
	Worn camshaft drive chain (rattle)	Adjust tensioner or replace chain.
	Worn big end bearings (whirring noise)	Fit replacement crankshaft assembly.
	Worn main bearings (rumble)	Fit new journal bearings and seals. Replace crankshaft assembly if centre bearings are worn.
Engine overheats and fades	Lubrication failure	Stop engine and check whether internal parts are receiving oil. Check oil level in crankcase.

43 Fault diagnosis - gearbox

Symptom	Cause	Remedy
Difficulty in engaging gears	Selector forks bent	Replace.
	Gear clusters not assembled correctly	Check gear cluster arrangement and position of thrust washers.
Machine jumps out of gear	Worn dogs on ends of gear pinions	Replace worn pinions.
	Stopper arms not seating correctly	Remove right hand crankcase cover and check stopper arm action.
Gear change lever does not return to original position	Broken return spring	Replace spring.
Kickstarter does not return when engine is turned over or started	Broken or poorly tensioned return spring	Replace spring or re-tension.
Kickstarter slips	Ratchet assembly worn	Part crankcase and replace all worn parts.

44 Fault diagnosis - clutch

Symptom	Cause	Remedy
Engine speed increases as shown by tachometer but machine does not respond	Clutch slip	Check clutch adjustment for free play at handlebar lever. Check thickness of inserted plates.
Difficulty in engaging gears. Gear changes jerky and machine creeps forward when clutch is withdrawn. Difficulty in selecting neutral	Clutch drag	Check clutch adjustment for too much free play. Check clutch drums for indentations in slots and clutch plates for burrs on tongues. Dress with file if damage not too great.
Clutch operation stiff	Damaged, trapped or frayed control cable	Check cable and replace if necessary. Make sure cable is lubricated and has no sharp bends.

Chapter 2 Fuel system and Lubrication

Contents

Specifications

	CB125	CB160	CB175/CD175
Fuel tank capacity		10.5 litres 2.3 Imp gallons	12 litres 2.2 Imp gallons
Engine oil		1 litre 1.76 Imp pints	1.5 litres 2.64 Imp pints
Carburettor(s)			
Make	Twin Keihin	Single Keihin, CD175 only	
Type		Piston valve	
Main jet	78	90	98 (96 CD175)
Air jet	1.2	150	150
Needle jet	2.59 - 0.6 x 8	2.6 x 3.5	2.6 x 3.8
Jet needle	T-18B	18331	2°30
Slow running jet	0.35	38	38

NOTE: Twin carburettors have identical jettings

1 General description

The fuel system comprises a petrol tank from which petrol is fed by gravity to the carburettor(s) via a petrol tap containing a filter bowl. The tap has three positions: 'on', 'off', and 'reserve', the latter providing a small amount of petrol after the main supply has run dry so that the machine will cover a short distance.

All models are fitted with twin carburettors of Keihin manufacture with the exception of the CD175 model which has only a single Keihin carburettor. These carburettors have integral float chambers and a manually operated choke. The administration of the correct petrol/air mixture is controlled by a conventional throttle slide and needle jet arrangement. A large capacity air cleaner, with a corrugated paper element, serves the dual purpose of supplying clean air to the carburettor intake and effectively silencing the intake roar.

Although the oil content, which is common to both engine and gearbox, is contained in a separate crankcase compartment, the lubrication system operates on the dry sump principle and utilises a plunger-type oil pump to provide a pressure feed. The oil passes through a centrifugal filter to a gallery in the upper crankcase where it separates into two paths. One feeds the overhead camshaft and rocker gear and returns by gravity via the camshaft chain tunnel; the other feeds the main bearings, big ends and gearbox bearings. All remaining parts are lubricated by splash and/or oil mist.

2 Petrol tank - removal and replacement

1 The petrol tank fitted to the CB175 and CD175 models is secured to the frame by means of a short channel that projects from the nose of the tank and engages with a rubber 'buffer' surrounding a pin welded to the frame, immediately behind the steering head. This arrangement is duplicated either side of the nose of the tank and the frame. The rear of the petrol tank has a projecting lip that engages with a rubber cushion below the nose of the dual seat. As a result, the petrol tank is entirely rubber mounted and has no mechanical means of fixing.

2 The petrol tank fitted to the CB125 and CB160 models is also rubber mounted at the front, using a variation of the fixing described in the previous paragraph. At the rear end of the tank a welded-on lug on each side serves as the anchor point for the tank. A bolt passes through these lugs and a short tube welded across the frame. It is necessary to slacken and remove the nut and the bolt itself before the tank can be freed.

3 Before the CD175 petrol tank can be lifted off the machine, it must first be drained of petrol, so that the pipe joining both halves of the tank can be detached. Do not omit to remove the pipe from the petrol tap to the carburettor float chamber.

4 When replacing the tank, reverse the procedure used for its removal.

3 Petrol tap - removal, dismantling and replacement

1   Before the petrol tap can be removed, it is first necessary to drain the tank. This is easily accomplished by removing the feed pipe from a carburettor float chamber and allowing the contents of the tank to drain into a clean receptacle with the tap turned to the 'reserve' position.

2   Detach the various feed pipes from the tap. The tap itself is retained to the underside of the petrol tank by a screw or screws, either through the flange of the outside body or within the tap, after the filter bowl has been removed, depending on the model. If access to the filter only is required there is no necessity to remove the tap body. It is held to the underside by a single screw.

3   There is a gasket between the body of the petrol tap and the underside of the tank which should be renewed whenever the tap is disturbed. If this precaution is not observed, it may prove difficult to obtain a leak-tight joint on reassembly.

4   If the tap lever leaks, there is no necessity to remove the main body of the tap from the petrol tank, even though there is still need to drain the tank. If the two screws in the lever surround are withdrawn, the complete lever assembly can be taken out and the packing behind the lever removed and replaced.

5   When reassembling the tap, reverse the procedure for dismantling. Use new gaskets and check that the filter gauze and filter bowl are clean, before refilling the petrol tank with petrol.

6   Check that the feed pipe(s) from the tap to the carburettor(s) are in good condition and that the push-on joints are still a good fit, irrespective of the retaining wire clips. If particles of rubber are found in the filter, replace the pipes, since this is an indication that the internal bore is breaking up.

3.2 Filter bowl unscrews from base of petrol tap

3.2a Filter element is accessible after filter bowl is removed

4 Carburettor(s) - removal

1   An identical method of mounting is used, irrespective of whether a single or twin carburettors are fitted. The mounting is of the flange fitting type, over studs that project from the cylinder head inlet ports in the case of the CB125 models. The CB160 model has an adaptor interposed between the inlet port and the carburettor flange, using the same method of attachment. It is customary to remove the carburettors complete with the adaptors. The CD175 model has only a single carburettor although this too has an adaptor fitted.

2   Before the carburettor(s) can be detached by removing the two flange nuts, it is necessary to unscrew the top(s) of the mixing chamber(s) and withdraw the throttle valve(s) with needle(s) attached. Remove the rubber hose(s) which connect the carburettor air intake(s) with the air cleaner(s). The hose is secured by a wire clip.

3   When twin carburettors are fitted, they are of identical specification although they are 'handed'. This is to ensure the throttle stop and pilot jet adjusting screws are on the outward facing side of the carburettor in each case to facilitate ease of adjustment.

4   Although the carburettors can be drawn off as a pair, they are joined together only by the rod that links both hand operated chokes. It is preferable to detach the split pin and washer through the linkage at the right hand carburettor, so that each carburettor is withdrawn as a separate unit. Take care not to lose the O ring seal which may be displaced from the flange mounting joint.

5 Carburettor(s) - dismantling and reassembly

1   Invert each carburettor and remove the float chamber by prising off the retaining clip. The twin float assembly can be lifted away after the hinge pin has been displaced, giving access to the float needle and needle seating. Place the float needle in a safe place until reassembly commences; it is minute and very easily lost. The float needle seating will unscrew from the mixing chamber body.

2   Note there is a gasket between the float chamber and the mixing chamber body which should not be disturbed unless it is damaged or has shown signs of leakage.

3   Check that the floats are in good condition and not punctured. Because they are made from brass, it is possible to effect a repair by soldering, but it is questionable whether such a repair can be justified other than in an emergency. The addition of solder will affect the weight of the float assembly and result in a different petrol level. Whenever possible, fit a new replacement.

4   The main jet is located in the centre of the oblong mixing chamber housing and screws into the carburettor body, at the same time locating the needle jet. The latter is a press fit and can be pressed downwards out of position, through the slide orifice. After a lengthy period of service, the needle jet will wear and give rise to an increase in petrol consumption. It is advisable to renew the needle jet periodically, in conjunction with the needle itself.

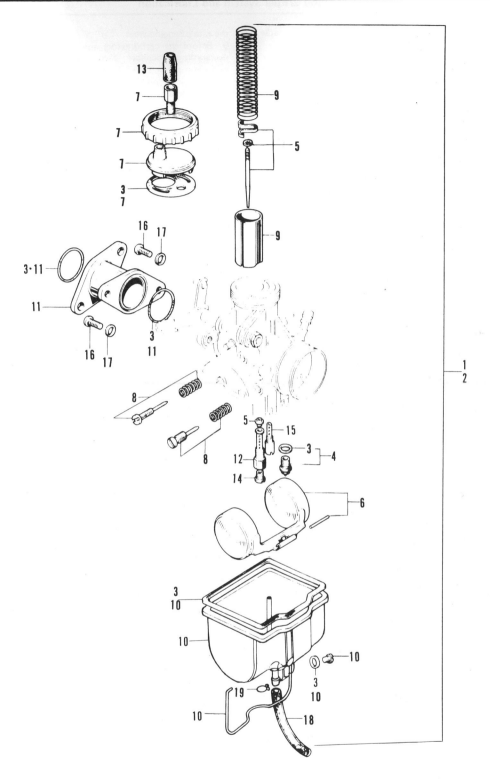

Fig 2.1 KEIHIN CARBURETTOR

1 Carburettor complete, right hand
2 Carburettor complete, left hand
3 Carburettor gasket set
4 Float needle seating
5 Needle and clip
6 Float assembly
7 Carburettor top assembly

8 Pilot jet screw and throttle stop screw
9 Throttle valve and spring
10 Float chamber assembly
11 Flange adaptor
12 Needle jet
13 Rubber cap

14 Main jet
15 Pilot jet
16 Carburettor flange screw - 2 off
17 Plain washer - 2 off
18 Overflow pipe
19 Pipe clip

renew the needle jet periodically, in conjunction with the needle itself.

5 The float needle seating will wear after lengthy service and should be closely examined with a magnifying glass. Wear usually takes the form of a ridge or groove, which will cause the float needle to seat imperfectly. Always renew the seating and float needle as a pair, especially since similar wear will almost certainly occur on the point of the needle.

6 The carburettor slides, or throttle valves, are attached to the cables that pass through the mixing chamber tops. The twist grip cable divides into two by means of a junction box normally hidden under the petrol tank, as a convenient means of actuating both carburettors simultaneously. Each slide has a return spring and the needle, suspended by means of a spring clip, from the centre. The needle is grooved, so that it can be either raised or lowered in order to vary the mixture strength.

7 The other jet threaded into the oblong mixing chamber is the pilot jet. This jet should be removed periodically and blown out with a jet of compressed air to ensure the tiny air passages are not obstructed by any sediment from the petrol.

8 The manually-operated chokes are unlikely to require attention throughout the normal service life of the machine. When the operating plungers are depressed, flaps are lowered into the carburettor air intake that cut off the supply of air and therefore give a much richer mixture for cold starting. The machine should never be run for any distance with the chokes closed or the excessively rich mixture will foul the spark plugs and wash the oil from the cylinder walls, greatly accelerating the rate of engine wear.

9 Before the carburettors are reassembled, using the reversed dismantling procedure, each should be cleaned out thoroughly using compressed air. Avoid using a piece of rag since there is always risk of particles of lint obstructing the internal passage-ways or the jet orifices.

10 Never use a piece of wire or any pointed metal object to clear a blocked jet. It is only too easy to enlarge the jet under these circumstances and increase the rate of petrol consumption. If compressed air is not available, a blast of air from a tyre pump will usually suffice.

11 Do not use excessive force when reassembling a carburettor because it is easy to shear a jet or some of the smaller screws. Furthermore, the carburettors are cast in a zinc-based alloy which itself does not have a high tensile strength. Take particular care when replacing the mixing chamber tops to ensure the needles align with the needle jets and that the top is not engaged cross-threaded.

12 Avoid overtightening the nuts that retain the carburettors or their adaptors to the cylinder heads. Overtightening will cause the flanges to bow, giving rise to mysterious air leaks and a permanently weak mixture. If the flange is bowed, it can be rubbed down until it is flat once again using a rotary motion and a sheet of emery cloth wrapped around a sheet of glass. Make sure no particles of emery grit enter the carburettors and that the O ring in the centre of each flange is replaced when the grinding operation is complete.

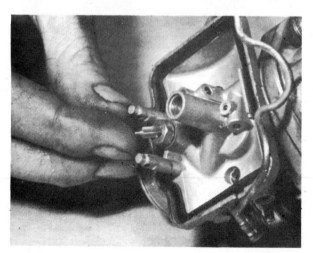

5.1 Prise off retaining clip to remove float chamber

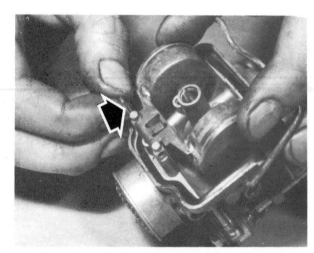

5.1a Float unit can be lifted away after removing hinge pin

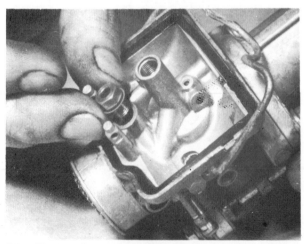

5.1b Float needle is tiny and easily lost

5.1c Float needle seating unscrews from main body of carburettor

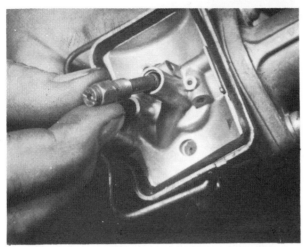

5.4 Main jet screws into base of needle jet

5.4a Main jet can be separated, if desired

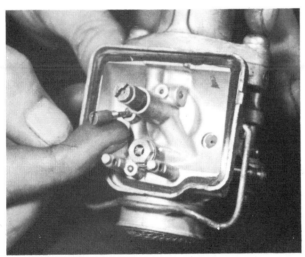

5.6 Pilot jet also screws into main body of carburettor

5.9 The carburettor float and mixing chambers fully dismantled

6.4 Adjust pilot jet and throttle stop screws together when arriving at final setting

6 Carburettors - adjustment

1 When adjustments are required it is best to regard each carburettor as a separate entity. Remove the spark plug from the cylinder which is not receiving attention so that only one cylinder will fire during the adjustments. Then change over and follow a similar routine.

2 Commence operations by checking the float level, which will involve detaching the carburettor concerned, inverting it and removing the float chamber bowl. If the float level is correct, the height of the float assembly above the carburettor body should be 27 mm (19.5 mm, CB125 and CB160 models) when the float arm and float needle have a clearance of 0.003 inch. To adjust this setting, bend the float arm.

3 Replace the carburettor and adjust the pilot jet screw until it is closed fully. Then turn it back approximately 1½ complete turns. Adjust the throttle stop screw, with the engine running, until a slow reliable tickover speed is achieved.

4 Re-adjust the pilot jet screw to see whether any improvement is gained, using the throttle stop to either raise or lower the engine speed. The objective is to obtain a slow, reliable tickover without having the pilot jet setting either too rich or too weak. The 1½ turns setting is normally near correct.

5 Stop the engine, replace the spark plug and lead, and then repeat the procedure with the other cylinder and carburettor, after first removing the spark plug from the cylinder which has just been checked.

6 When both spark plugs are reconnected and the engine started, it is probable that the tickover speed will be too high. This can be remedied by slackening both throttle stop screws an identical amount, normally only a very small movement. If a tachometer is fitted, the recommended tickover speed is 1200 rpm.

7 These adjustments must always be made with the engine at normal running temperature and with both air cleaners attached, otherwise completely false settings will be obtained.

7 Synchronising the carburettors

1 Power output will be unbalanced unless both carburettors work in perfect harmony with each other. Many cases of poor performance and low power output can be traced to carburettors which are out of phase with each other.

2 Start by checking whether both carburettor slides rise and fall simultaneously. They should both commence to lift at the same time; if there is any lag, adjust the carburettor concerned by means of the cable adjuster in the mixing chamber top. It will be necessary to temporarily detach the air cleaner hoses to observe the slide action.

3 Slowly close the throttle and check that both slides re-enter the carburettor bores at the same time. If they do not, adjust by means of the cable adjuster concerned until they are in phase. Check that both slides close fully when the throttle is shut.

4 Before reconnecting the air cleaner hoses, check also that the hand operated chokes are in phase with one another. Adjustment is made by means of the threaded rod between both plungers, after the split pin and washer of the right hand carburettor have been temporarily disconnected.

5 If carburettor adjustments are required, they should be made BEFORE the carburettors are synchronised. Always make the synchronising adjustments with the engine warm to obviate the risk of a false setting.

8 Carburettor settings

1 Some of the carburettor settings, such as the sizes of the needle jets, main jets and needle positions etc, are pre-determined by the manufacturer. Under normal circumstances it is unlikely that these settings will require modification, even though there is provision made. If a change appears necessary, it can often be attributed to a developing engine fault.

2 As an approximate guide the pilot jet setting controls engine speed up to 1/8 throttle. The throttle slide cut-a-way controls engine speed from 1/8 to 1/4 throttle and the position of the needle in the slide from 1/4 to 3/4 throttle. The size of the main jet is responsible for engine speed at the final 3/4 to full throttle. It should be added however that these are only guide lines. There is no clearly defined demarcation line due to a certain amount of overlap that occurs between the carburettor components involved.

3 Always err slightly on the side of a rich mixture, since a weak mixture will cause the engine to overheat. Reference to Chapter 3 will show how the condition of the spark plugs can be interpreted with some experience as a reliable guide to carburettor mixture strength.

9 Exhaust system - cleaning

1 Unlike a two-stroke, the exhaust system does not require such frequent attention because the exhaust gases are usually of a less oily nature. However, instances may occur when it is necessary to withdraw the baffles from the silencers in order to clean them, especially if the engine is approaching the time for a rebore and is burning oil.

3 Each baffle tube assembly is retained by a single crosshead

screw, located within the end of each silencer. When the screw is removed, the baffle tube can be withdrawn. There is no necessity to remove the exhaust system from the machine, during this operation.

3 The baffles should be cleaned with a wire brush, or if the carbon is particularly oily, by washing with a petrol/paraffin mix. In an extreme case, a blow lamp can be used to burn off any heavy accumulation of carbon.

4 Do not run the machine with the exhaust baffles detached, or with a quite different type of silencer fitted. The standard production silencers have been designed to give the best possible performance, whilst subduing the exhaust note to an acceptable level. Although a modified exhaust system, or one without baffles, may give the illusion of greater speed as a result of the changed exhaust note, the chances are that performance will have suffered accordingly.

5 When replacing the baffles, make sure the crosshead retaining screws are tightened fully. If they work loose, the baffle tubes may fall out whilst the machine is in motion. Note that the CB175/CD175K6 models do not have detachable baffles.

10.2 Pull off side covers for access to air cleaners

10.2a Centre nut retains moulded plastics cover over air cleaner element

10.3 Remove both fixing bolts and intake hose to release element unit

10.3a Element is lifted away complete with metal housing

10 Air cleaners - dismantling, servicing and reassembly

1   Each carburettor has its own air cleaner, which is attached to the right and left hand side of the machine, according to the carburettor connection. The CD175 model, which has only a single carburettor, has the air cleaner mounted on the left hand side of the machine, beneath the left hand side cover.

2   To gain access to the air cleaner element, pull off the side cover immediately below the dual seat. It is a push-in fit, through rubber grommets. Remove the centre nut and washer which retains the moulded plastics cover over the air cleaner element and lift the cover away.

3   The air cleaner element is contained within a metal box which is bolted to the subframe of the machine. Remove both bolts and slacken the hose clip or wire clip around the rubber tube leading to the carburettor air intake. The element, which is integral with its metal housing, can then be lifted away. The CB125 and CB160 models have a slightly different arrangement; the element is exposed immediately the side covers are detached.

4   To clean the element, tap it lightly to loosen the accumulation of dust and then use a soft brush to sweep the dust away. Alternatively, compressed air can be blown into the element from the inside. Remember the element is composed of

corrugated paper and is easily damaged if handled roughly.

5   If the element is damp or oily, it must be renewed. A damp or oily element will have a restrictive effect on the breathing of the carburettor and will almost certainly affect engine performance.

6   On no account run without the air cleaners attached, or with the element missing. The jetting of the carburettors takes into account the presence of the air cleaners and engine performance will be seriously affected if this balance is upset.

7   To replace the elements, reverse the dismantling procedure. Make sure that the inlet hoses to the carburettors are not kinked, split or otherwise damaged, otherwise air leaks will occur and affect the carburation.

11 Engine lubrication

1   The engine oil, which is common also to the gearbox, is contained within a crankcase compartment, formed by the right hand outer cover. This compartment holds 1.5 litres of oil (1 litre, CB125 and CB160 models) and has a dipstick integral with the filler cap. When checking the oil level, the cap should be rested on the end of its screw thread and not screwed home into the filler orifice.

2   The lubrication system works on the dry sump principle. The plunger type oil pump, which is driven from an eccentric behind the clutch, picks up oil from the crankcase compartment which passes to the upper crankcase through an oilway in the cover of the centrifugal oil filter. Impurities in the oil are removed by the centrifugal force of the rotating filter and retained within the outer casing until the filter is cleaned out periodically. The clean oil is fed to the upper crankcase to the crankshaft bearings. Where it enters the right and left hand crankshaft outer rings, it divides into two separate channels. One lubricates the roller bearing and the other enters the crankshaft to lubricate the big ends. This is a pressure feed; the remainder of the lower engine components are lubricated on the splash principle.

3   The oil passageway in the upper crankcase also divides into two at the rear of the cylinder block. On the right hand side, oil travels up the rearmost cylinder holding down stud to provide a feed to the cylinder head for lubricating the camshaft and the rocker gear. Excess oil drains back via the camshaft chain tunnel to the crankcase. The other route enters the gearbox via a crankcase drilling to lubricate the gearbox mainshaft and pinions. The remainder of the gearbox components are lubricated by splash from the oil which drains into the base.

12 Centrifugal oil filter - dismantling, cleaning and replacing

1   Access to the centrifugal oil filter is provided in the form of a circular detachable plate in the right hand crankcase cover, retained by three crosshead screws. The cover contains internal oilways and the screws are offset so that the cover cannot be replaced in the wrong position.

2   The cover seats on an O ring seal which must be in good condition. If there is any question about the condition of the ring, it should be renewed.

3   The filter cover is retained by a central crosshead screw. Remove the screw and draw off the cover, using a pair of long nosed pliers on the grips provided. The cover is a tight fit, due to the O ring seal around its periphery. When the cover is released, a small amount of oil will flow out and it is advisable to place a container below to catch this oil.

4   Wash the oil filter cover and the interior of the oil filter body with petrol, removing any sediment that may be present. Dry the cover and filter body, then replace the cover, after checking that the O ring seal around the periphery is in good order.

5   Note that the cover locates with internally-cast grooves inside the filter body. The cover will not seat correctly if the tongued portion fails to engage with these grooves. Refit the centre screw and tighten it fully.

6   Before replacing the outer cover which is retained by three crosshead screws, check that the pressure release valve in the centre moves freely. The valve is spring-loaded and should press

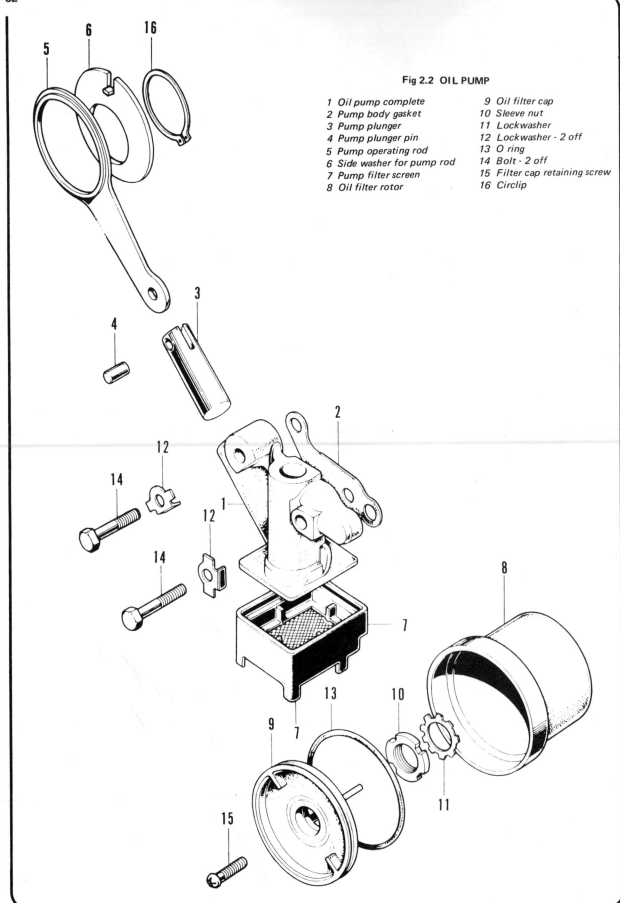

Fig 2.2 OIL PUMP

1 Oil pump complete
2 Pump body gasket
3 Pump plunger
4 Pump plunger pin
5 Pump operating rod
6 Side washer for pump rod
7 Pump filter screen
8 Oil filter rotor

9 Oil filter cap
10 Sleeve nut
11 Lockwasher
12 Lockwasher - 2 off
13 O ring
14 Bolt - 2 off
15 Filter cap retaining screw
16 Circlip

inwards. This check is important because if the valve sticks in the 'in' position, THERE IS NO OIL PRESSURE IN THE LUBRICATION SYSTEM.

7   As a final check, make sure the oilways in the cover line up with those in the right hand crankcase cover before the three crosshead screws are inserted and the cover tightened.

13 Oil pump

1   The oil pump works on the plunger principle and is driven from an eccentric behind the clutch. It is unlikely that the pump will require attention during the normal working life of the machine, unless the gauze at the base of the pump is blocked or oil shortage causes wear in the form of increased clearance between the plunger and the plunger bore. In this latter case, a new pump should be fitted.

2   Always fit a new gasket behind the pump whenever it is disturbed and check that the oilways align accurately. Make sure that the two retaining bolts are tight and secured by tab washers.

14 Checking the oil circulation

1   After an engine has been rebuilt, or the oil pump disturbed, it is advisable to check the oil circulation. If there is no pressure, the top half of the engine will be starved of oil, leading to a seizure.

2   To check the oil circulation, remove the two acorn nuts at the extreme right and left hand rear of the cylinder head cover. Since oil travels up the outer holding studs, it can be seen emerging from the cylinder head cover, around the studs, when the engine is running. Do not omit to retighten the acorn nuts fully after carrying out this check.

15 Fault diagnosis

Symptom	Cause	Remedy
Engine gradually fades and stops	Fuel starvation	Check vent hole in filler cap. Sediment in filter bowl or blocking float needle. Dismantle and clean.
Engine runs badly. Black smoke from exhausts	Carburettor flooding	Dismantle and clean carburettor. Check for punctured float or sticking float needle.
Engine lacks response and overheats	Weak mixture Air cleaner disconnected Modified silencer has upset carburation	Check for partial blockage in carburettors. Reconnect. Check hoses for splits. Replace with original.
Engine loses power and gets noisy	Lubrication failure	Stop engine immediately and do not re-run until fault is located and remedied.

Castrol GRADES

Castrol Engine Oils

Castrol GTX

An ultra high performance SAE 20W/50 motor oil which exceeds the latest API MS requirements and manufacturers' specifications. Castrol GTX with liquid tungsten† generously protects engines at the extreme limits of performance, and combines both good cold starting with oil consumption control. Approved by leading car makers.

Castrol XL 20/50

Contains liquid tungsten†; well suited to the majority of conditions giving good oil consumption control in both new and old cars.

Castrolite (Multi-grade)

This is the lightest multi-grade oil of the Castrol motor oil family containing liquid tungsten†. It is best suited to ensure easy winter starting and for those car models whose manufacturers specify lighter weight oils.

Castrol Grand Prix

An SAE 50 engine oil for use where a heavy, full-bodied lubricant is required.

Castrol Two-Stroke-Four

A premium SAE 30 motor oil possessing good detergency characteristics and corrosion inhibitors, coupled with low ash forming tendency and excellent anti-scuff properties. It is suitable for all two-stroke motor-cycles, and for two-stroke and small four-stroke horticultural machines.

Castrol CR (Multi-grade)

A high quality engine oil of the SAE-20W/30 multi-grade type, suited to mixed fleet operations.

Castrol CRI 10, 20, 30

Primarily for diesel engines, a range of heavily fortified, fully detergent oils, covering the requirements of DEF 2101-D and Supplement 1 specifications.

Castrol CRB 20, 30

Primarily for diesel engines, heavily fortified, fully detergent oils, covering the requirements of MIL-L-2104B.

Castrol R 40

Primarily designed and developed for highly stressed racing engines. Castrol 'R' should not be mixed with any other oil nor with any grade of Castrol.
†*Liquid Tungsten is an oil soluble long chain tertiary alkyl primary amine tungstate covered by British Patent No. 882,295.*

Castrol Gear Oils

Castrol Hypoy (90 EP)

A light-bodied powerful extreme pressure gear oil for use in hypoid rear axles and in some gearboxes.

Castrol Gear Oils (continued)

Castrol Hypoy Light (80 EP)

A very light-bodied powerful extreme pressure gear oil for use in hypoid rear axles in cold climates and in some gearboxes.

Castrol Hypoy B (90 EP)

A light-bodied powerful extreme pressure gear oil that complies with the requirements of the MIL-L-2105B specification, for use in certain gearboxes and rear axles.

Castrol Hi-Press (140 EP)

A heavy-bodied extreme pressure gear oil for use in spiral bevel rear axles and some gearboxes.

Castrol ST (90)

A light-bodied gear oil with fortifying additives

Castrol D (140)

A heavy full-bodied gear oil with fortifying additives.

Castrol Thio-Hypoy FD (90 EP)

A light-bodied powerful extreme pressure gear oil. This is a special oil for running-in certain hypoid gears.

Automatic Transmission Fluids

Castrol TQF

(Automatic Transmission Fluid)

Approved for use in all Borg-Warner Automatic Transmission Units. Castrol TQF also meets Ford specification M2C 33F.

Castrol TQ Dexron®

(Automatic Transmission Fluid)

Complies with the requirements of Dexron® Automatic Transmission Fluids as laid down by General Motors Corporation.

Castrol Greases

Castrol LM

A multi-purpose high melting point lithium based grease approved for most automotive applications including chassis and wheel bearing lubrication.

Castrol MS3

A high melting point lithium based grease containing molybdenum disulphide.

Castrol BNS

A high melting point grease for use where recommended by certain manufacturers in front wheel bearings when disc brakes are fitted.

Castrol Greases (continued)

Castrol CL

A semi-fluid calcium based grease, which is both waterproof and adhesive, intended for chassis lubrication.

Castrol Medium

A medium consistency calcium based grease.

Castrol Heavy

A heavy consistency calcium based grease.

Castrol PH

A white grease for plunger housings and other moving parts on brake mechanisms. *It must NOT be allowed to come into contact with brake fluid when applied to the moving parts of hydraulic brakes.*

Castrol Graphited Grease

A graphited grease for the lubrication of transmission chains.

Castrol Under-Water Grease

A grease for the under-water gears of outboard motors.

Anti-Freeze

Castrol Anti-Freeze

Contains anti-corrosion additives with ethylene glycol. Recommended for the cooling systems of all petrol and diesel engines.

Speciality Products

Castrol Girling Damper Oil Thin

The oil for Girling piston type hydraulic dampers.

Castrol Shockol

A light viscosity oil for use in some piston type shock absorbers and in some hydraulic systems employing synthetic rubber seals. It must not be used in braking systems.

Castrol Penetrating Oil

A leaf spring lubricant possessing a high degree of penetration and providing protection against rust.

Castrol Solvent Flushing Oil

A light-bodied solvent oil, designed for flushing engines, rear axles, gearboxes and gearcasings.

Castrollo

An upper cylinder lubricant for use in the proportion of 1 fluid ounce to two gallons of fuel.

Everyman Oil

A light-bodied machine oil containing anti-corrosion additives for both general use and cycle lubrication.

Chapter 3 Ignition System

Contents

Specifications

	CB125	CB160	CB175/CD175
Spark plugs			
Make		NGK	
Size		12 mm	
Type		D-8HS	
Gap		0.6 to 0.7 mm (0.024 to 0.028 in)	
Equivalents		Champion P-7, Lodge H-12, KLG TW75	
Ignition timing		5º BTDC (35º fully advanced) - all models	
Contact breaker gap		0.3 to 0.4 mm (0.012 to 0.016 in) - all models	

1 General description

The spark necessary to ignite the petrol/air mixture in the combustion chambers is derived from a battery and a single ignition coil. A single contact breaker operates in conjunction with a twin lobe cam to determine the exact moment at which the spark will occur in each cylinder. When the contact breaker points separate the low tension circuit is broken and a high tension voltage is developed by the coil which jumps the air gap across the points of the spark plug due to fire and ignites the mixture.

The AC generator attached to the extreme left hand end of the crankshaft generates an alternating current which is rectified and used to charge the 12 volt battery. The rectifier is located under the dual seat, in close proximity to the battery, and the ignition coil is mounted immediately behind the steering head, covered by the petrol tank. The contact breaker is attached to the left hand end of the overhead camshaft, within a separate compartment sealed with a chromium plated end cover. The circuit is actuated by a switch on the left hand side of the machine, below the nose of the petrol tank, which switches on the ignition and operates the lights, both for running and parking.

2 Crankshaft alternator - checking the output

Some indication of the output from the alternator mounted the end of the crankshaft can be obtained by removing the

wires from the positive terminal of the battery (one red/white wire and one coloured red completely) and reconnecting these two wires to the negative terminal of an ammeter with a 0 to 5 amp range. The positive terminal of the ammeter should be connected to the vacant positive terminal of the battery and the engine started. If the alternator is functioning correctly, the following ammeter readings should be obtained:

| Lights | Initial charging rpm | | 5000 rpm | |
	Rpm	Battery voltage	Charge rate	Battery voltage
Off	2400	13.2V	1.8A	14V
On (full beam)	2800	13.2V	0.8A	14V
On (dipped beam)	2200	13.2V	1.5A	14V

Battery voltage is measured during the test by connecting a 0 to 15 volt voltmeter between the battery positive terminal and a convenient earthing point on the machine.

2 If much lower ammeter or voltmeter readings are obtained, it will be necessary to check the three main components of the charging circuit, namely the generator, selenium rectifier and the battery. More sophisticated test equipment of the multimeter type is required in this instance and since the average owner will not have access to this equipment or instruction in its use, it is advisable to entrust this type of check to a Honda agent or an auto-electrical expert. This is particularly necessary in the case of the rectifier which is damaged irreparably if a reverse flow of current should occur.

3 Ignition coil - checking

1 The ignition coil is a sealed unit, designed to give long service without need for attention. It is located within the top frame tubes, immediately to the rear of the steering head assembly. If a weak spark and difficult starting causes the performance of the coil to be suspect, it should be tested by a Honda agent or an auto-electrical expert who will have the appropriate test equipment. A faulty coil must be replaced; it is not possible to effect a satisfactory repair.

2 A defective condenser in the contact breaker circuit can give the illusion of a defective coil and for this reason it is advisable to investigate the condition of the condenser before condemning the ignition coil. Refer to Section 6 of this Chapter for the appropriate details.

4 Contact breaker - adjustments

1 To gain access to the contact breaker assembly, it is necessary to detach the chromium plated cover retained by two crosshead screws to the left hand side of the cylinder head casting.

2 Rotate the engine slowly by means of the kickstarter until the points are in the fully-open position. Examine the faces of the contacts; if they are pitted or burnt, it will be necessary to remove them for further attention, as described in Section 5 of this Chapter.

3 Adjustment is carried out by slackening the two screws which retain the fixed contact breaker point and inserting a screwdriver in the adjusting screw slot provided. Turn the adjusting screw in the appropriate direction until the gap is within the range 0.3 to 0.4 mm (0.012 to 0.016 in) and then retighten the two retaining screws. It is imperative that the points are open FULLY whilst this adjustment is made, or a false reading will result.

4 Repeat this adjustment when the points are opened by the second lobe of the contact breaker cam. If the cam is accurate, no further adjustment should be required. If there is only a very minor discrepancy the error can be tolerated but if one lobe provides a reading outside the limits of adjustment, the cam itself is unbalanced and must be replaced.

5 Before replacing the cover and gasket, place a slight smear of grease on the contact breaker cam and a few drops of thin oil on the felt wick which lubricates the surface of the cam. Do not over-lubricate or there is a chance of oil working on to the contact breaker points.

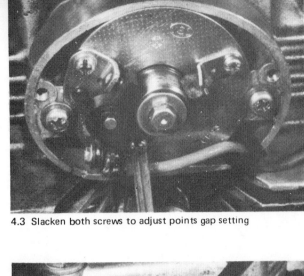

4.3 Slacken both screws to adjust points gap setting

4.3a Small screw provides convenient means of adjustment

4.1 Contact breaker assembly is behind left hand chromium plated cover

4.3b Always double check gap after tightening setting screws

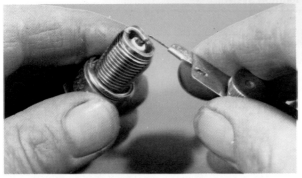

Spark plug maintenance: Checking plug gap with feeler gauges

Altering the plug gap. Note use of correct tool

Spark plug conditions: A brown, tan or grey firing end is indicative of correct engine running conditions and the selection of the appropriate heat rating plug

White deposits have accumulated from excessive amounts of oil in the combustion chamber or through the use of low quality oil. Remove deposits or a hot spot may form

Black sooty deposits indicate an over-rich fuel/air mixture, or a malfunctioning ignition system. If no improvement is obtained, try one grade hotter plug

Wet, oily carbon deposits form an electrical leakage path along the insulator nose, resulting in a misfire. The cause may be a badly worn engine or a malfunctioning ignition system

A blistered white insulator or melted electrode indicates over-advanced ignition timing or a malfunctioning cooling system. If correction does not prove effective, try a colder grade plug

A worn spark plug not only wastes fuel but also overloads the whole ignition system because the increased gap requires higher voltage to initiate the spark. This condition can also affect air pollution

4.5 Oil felt wick occasionally to lubricate cam

5 Contact breaker points - removal, renovation and replacement

1 If the contact breaker points are burned, pitted or badly worn, they should be removed for dressing. If it is necessary to remove a substantial amount of material before the faces can be restored, the points should be replaced without question.

2 To remove the contact breaker points, detach the circlip which secures the moving contact to the pin on which it pivots. Remove the nut and bolt that secures the flexible lead wire to the end of contact return spring, noting the arrangement of the insulating washers so that they are replaced in their correct order during reassembly. Lift the moving contact off the pivot, away from the assembly.

3 The fixed contact is removed by unscrewing the two screws which retain the contact to the contact breaker baseplate.

4 The points should be dressed with an oilstone or fine emery cloth. Keep them absolutely square throughout the dressing operation, otherwise they will make angular contact on re-assembly and rapidly burn away.

5 Replace the contacts by reversing the dismantling procedure, making sure that the insulating washers are replaced in the correct order. It is advantageous to apply a thin smear of grease to the pivot pin, prior to replacement of the moving contact arm.

6 Check, and if necessary, re-adjust the contact breaker gap when the points are fully opened by either lobe of the cam.

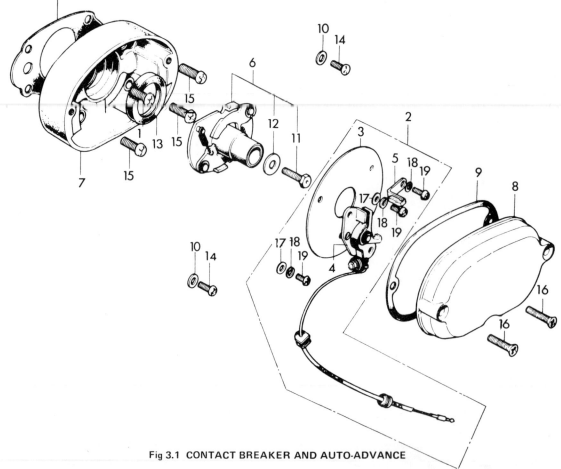

Fig 3.1 CONTACT BREAKER AND AUTO-ADVANCE

1 Gasket, left hand side cover	8 Contact breaker cover	14 Contact breaker plate lock screw - 2 off
2 Contact breaker assembly	9 Gasket for cover	15 Side cover retaining screws - 4 off
3 Contact breaker baseplate	10 Contact breaker lockwasher - 2 off	16 Contact breaker cover screws - 2 off
4 Contact breaker points	11 Bolt for contact breaker cam and	17 Plain washer - 2 off
5 Felt lubricating pad	auto-advance rotor	18 Spring washer - 2 off
6 Auto-advance rotor and cam	12 Washer	19 Screw - 3 off
7 Left hand side cover	13 Oil seal	

5.2 Remove lead wire and circlip to detach moving contact

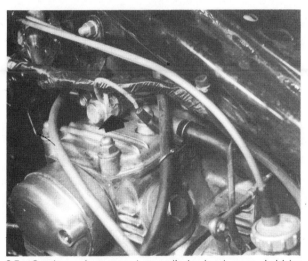

6.5 Condenser is mounted on cylinder head cover, held by holding down nut

7.2 F mark must align with pointer as points separate

6 Condenser - removal and replacement

1   A condenser is included in the contact breaker circuity to prevent arcing across the contact breaker points as they separate. The condenser is connected in parallel with the points and if a fault develops, ignition failure is liable to occur.

2   If the engine proves difficult to start, or misfiring occurs, it is possible that the condenser is at fault. To check, separate the contact breaker points by hand when the ignition is switched on. If a spark occurs across the points and they have a blackened and burnt appearance, the condenser can be regarded as unserviceable.

3   It is not possible to check the condenser without the appropriate test equipment. In view of the low cost involved, it is preferable to fit a new replacement and observe the effect on engine performance.

4   Because the condenser and contact breaker assembly is common to both cylinders, it is highly improbable that a faulty condenser will give rise to a misfire on one cylinder only. In such a case it is advisable to seek the source of the trouble elsewhere, possibly in some other part of the ignition circuit or the carburettor.

5   The condenser is mounted on the cylinder head cover by means of a metal clamp soldered to its body. The clip is clamped under one of the acorn nuts fitted to the cylinder and cylinder head holding down studs. Since this fitting provides the earth connection of the condenser, it follows that the clip should make good contact with the cylinder head cover and be tightened fully. The electrical connection between the condenser and the contact breaker assembly is kept clear of the cylinder head fins by means of a small rubber grommet which attaches to the fins and provides a means of permanent location.

7 Ignition timing - checking and resetting

1   In order to check the accuracy of the ignition timing, it is first necessary to remove the contact breaker cover and the circular cover from the left hand crankcase cover which gives access to the generator rotor. It will be observed that the rotor is inscribed with two lines marked 'T' and 'F' and that there is a small pointer close to the rotor which also has an inscribed line.

2   If the ignition timing is correct, the 'F' line will coincide exactly with the line scribed on the pointer, when the contact breaker points are just commencing to separate. In order to check both cylinders, it is necessary to turn the rotor one complete revolution (360º) so that the reading on the other cylinder is obtained.

3   If there is a minor discrepancy between the two readings, it is permissible to 'share' the error, so that both cylinders fire at exactly the same setting. Some variation is almost inevitable, unless the contact breaker cam has been manufactured to an unusually high standard of accuracy. The magnitude of the error is however rarely sufficient to cause any problems, especially if the error is shared, as suggested.

4   To adjust the position of the contact breaker points relative to the cam, slacken the two crosshead screws at the periphery of the contact breaker baseplate. The whole baseplate can then be rotated either clockwise or anti-clockwise until the points commence to separate as the timing marks on the rotor coincide.

5   It cannot be overstressed that optimum performance depends on the accuracy with which the ignition timing is set. Even a small error can cause a marked reduction in performance and the possibility of engine damage, as the result of overheating. The contact breaker gap must be checked and if necessary reset for both lobes of the cam BEFORE the accuracy of the ignition timing is verified since adjustments made at a later stage will affect the accuracy of the setting.

6   Although the base of the contact breaker cam forms part of the integral automatic ignition advance mechanism, the ignition is timed when the unit is in the fully retarded position (balance weights unextended).

8 Automatic ignition advance - examination

1 The automatic ignition advance mechanism rarely requires attention, although it is advisable to examine it periodically, when the contact breaker is receiving attention. It is retained by a small bolt and washer through the centre of the integral contact breaker cam and can be pulled off the end of the camshaft when the contact breaker plate is removed.

2 The unit comprises spring loaded balance weights, which move outwards against the spring tension as centrifugal force increases. The balance weights must move freely on their pivots and be rust-free. The tension springs must also be in good condition. Keep the pivots lubricated and make sure the balance weights move easily, without binding. Most problems arise as a result of condensation within the engine, which causes the unit to rust and balance weight movement to be restricted.

3 When replacing the unit, make sure that either keyway aligns accurately with the pin through the end of the camshaft. The unit will not fit the camshaft correctly if alignment is incorrect and the ignition timing will be badly out of phase.

9 Spark plugs - checking and resetting the gaps

1 A matched pair of 12 mm short reach spark plugs are fitted to the Honda 125, 160 and 175 cc twin cylinder models.

2 All models are fitted with NGK type D-8HS spark plugs as standard, gapped within the range 0.6 to 0.7 mm (0.024 to 0.028 in). Certain operating conditions may indicate a change in spark plug grade; the type recommended by the manufacturer gives the best, all-round service.

3 Reference to the Specifications section of this Chapter shows the alternative recommendations of British spark plug manufacturers. Always use the grade of plug recommended, to obviate the risk of ignition problems.

4 Check the gap of the plug points during every 3 monthly or 2000 mile service. To reset the gap, bend the outer electrode to bring it closer to the centre electrode and check that a 0.6 mm (0.024 in) feeler gauge can be inserted. Never bend the central electrode or the insulator will crack, causing engine damage if particles fall in whilst the engine is running.

5 With some experience, the condition of the spark plug electrodes and insulator can be used as a reliable guide to engine operating conditions. See the accompanying diagram.

6 Always carry a spare pair of spark plugs of the recommended grade. In the rare event of plug failure, they will enable the engine to be restarted.

7 Beware of over-tightening the spark plugs, otherwise there is risk of stripping the threads from the aluminium alloy cylinder heads. The plugs should be sufficiently tight to seat firmly on their copper sealing washers, and no more. Use a spanner which is a good fit to prevent the spanner from slipping and breaking the insulator.

8 If the threads in the cylinder head strip as a result of over-tightening the spark plugs, it is possible to reclaim the head by the use of a Helicoil thread insert. This is a cheap and convenient method of replacing the threads; most motor cycle dealers operate a service of this nature at an economic price.

9 Make sure the plug insulating caps are a good fit and have their rubber seals. They should also be kept clean to prevent tracking. These caps contain the suppressors that eliminate both radio and TV interference.

10 Fault diagnosis

Symptom	Cause	Remedy
Engine will not start	Faulty ignition switch	Operate switch several times in case contacts are dirty. If lights and other electrics function, switch may need replacement.
	Starter motor not working	Discharged battery. Use kickstarter until battery is recharged.
	Short circuit in wiring	Check whether fuse is intact. Eliminate fault before switching on again.
Engine misfires	Faulty condenser in ignition circuit	Replace condenser and retest.
	Fouled spark plug	Replace plug and have original cleaned.
	Poor spark due to generator failure and discharging battery	Check output from generator. Remove and recharge battery.
Engine lacks power and overheats	Retarded ignition timing	Check timing and also contact breaker gap. Check whether auto-advance mechanism has jammed.
Engine 'fades' when under load	Pre-ignition	Check grade of plugs fitted; use recommended grades only. Verify whether lubrication system has pressure.

Chapter 4 Frame and Forks

Contents

1 General description

Two types of frame are employed for these Hondas. The CB175, CB160 and early CD175A models (1967-1969) models have a frame of the spine type in which there is no front down tube from the steering head to the crankcase of the engine unit. The CB175 and CD175 models share a common frame of the full cradle type, in which the engine unit is supported by duplex tubes at the base of the crankcase and by the conventional down tube running from the base of the steering head to this lower cradle.

The differences in frame layout necessitate different methods of engine mounting. The CB125 and CB160 engine units are mounted by means of lugs cast into the rear of the upper and lower crankcases and by plates welded along the lower frame tubes that extend rearwards from the base of the steering head and match up with lugs on the cylinder head cover. These engines are easily recognised by their 30° inclination from the vertical. The CB175 and CD175 engine units have only an 8° inclination and have cast-in lugs on the front of the crankcase which serve as attachment points for the short front engine mounting plates used in conjunction with the full cradle frame. In view of these basic differences, there is no easy means of transposing the engine units.

The forks have certain basic similarities in their mode of construction, although they are by no means identical in detail. The method used for dismantling and reassembly is however broadly the same as reference to the following text will show.

2 Front forks - removal from the frame

1 It is unlikely that the front forks will have to be removed from the frame as a complete unit, unless the steering head assembly requires attention or if the machine suffers frontal damage in an accident.

2 Commence operations by removing either the control cables from the handlebar levers or the levers complete with control cables still attached. The shape of the handlebars and the length of the cables will probably determine which method is to be preferred.

3 Detach the handlebars from the fork top yoke. They are retained by a pair of split clamps which, when removed, will free the handlebars. On some models it may first be necessary to remove the steering damper assembly. The damper knob, complete with rod, can be unscrewed from the friction discs at the base of the steering head column by turning it in an anti-clockwise direction, then lifting it away.

4 Detach the headlamp unit complete, disconnecting the internal wiring at the snap connectors provided. Reconnection at a later stage is made easy by the colour coding used for the wires. On models other than the CB175 it will be necessary to disconnect the speedometer drive cable and the tachometer drive cable (when fitted) from the speedometer/tachometer head contained within the headlamp shell. On the CB175 model, these instruments are connected to a mounting plate across the fork top yoke which is released when the bolts are withdrawn from the top of each fork leg.

5 If the machine is not already on its centre stand, support it in this fashion on a firm, level surface. Balance the machine so that the front wheel is well clear of the ground.

6 Remove the speedometer drive cable from the brake plate of the front wheel by unscrewing the coupling or by withdrawing the crosshead screw which retains the cable in position - the method of attachment depending on the model. Remove the front brake cable from the linkage on the end of the brake operating arm. The cable can then be pulled from the cable stop on the brake plate and freed completely, after unscrewing the adjuster.

7 The wheel can now be released from the forks by first releasing the bolt through the brake torque arm, then pulling out the front wheel spindle after releasing the split pin through the extreme right hand end and slackening the clamp bolt through the lower end of the left hand fork leg. If the right hand fork leg has a split clamp arrangement at the end, it may also be necessary to slacken off the clamp in order to free the end of the spindle. Note that in the case of the CB175 and CD175 models, the wheel spindle unscrews from the right hand fork leg (right hand thread). The CD175 model does not have a front brake

plate torque arm. A channel in the brake plate engages with a projection on the left hand fork leg.

8   Remove the front wheel, complete with brake plate assembly, and then the front mudguard which is secured to the inside of each fork leg by two bolts and washers.

9   Unscrew and remove the bolt in the top of each fork leg and the nut above the top yoke. The yoke can now be pulled off the steering head column, using a rawhide mallet to displace it initially. Hit with a series of sharp taps from the underside.

10 There is a sleeve nut below the yoke in the centre of the steering head column which must be unscrewed from the head stem to release the forks. The forks will drop downwards as the sleeve nut is unscrewed and it is advisable to wrap a piece of rag around the lower steering head bearing to catch the uncaged ball bearings as they are displaced. When the sleeve nut is unscrewed completely from the head stem, the complete fork unit can be lifted away after it is withdrawn from the lower end of the steering head. The upper steering head bearings will remain in position, especially if they are well greased.

2.6 Release brake cable from brake operating arm ...

2.6a ... then unscrew adjuster from brake plate and detach cable completely

2.6b Crosshead screw retains speedometer drive cable

2.7 Remove split pin through wheel spindle

2.7a Detach lower end of brake torque arm from brake plate

2.8 Front mudguard is bolted to inside of fork legs

2.9 Remove bolt from top of each fork leg

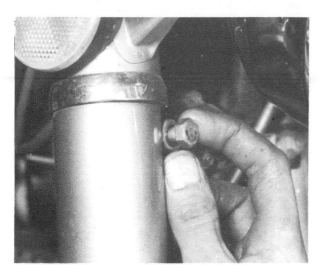

3.2 Slacken pinch bolts in lower fork yoke

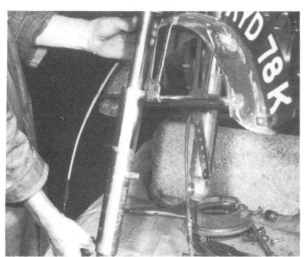

3.2a Fork leg can now be withdrawn downwards for complete dismantling

3 Front forks - dismantling

1 It is advisable to dismantle each fork leg separately using an identical procedure. There is less chance of unwittingly exchanging parts if this approach is adopted. Commence by draining the fork legs; there is a drain plug in each, above and to the rear of the wheel spindle housing.

2 Slacken the pinch bolt through each side of the lower fork yoke and if necessary, use a stout screwdriver to spread the slot when each pinch bolt has been removed in order to free the grip around the fork stanchions. The fork leg will then pull away from the lower yoke, after the upper covers have been lifted off.

3 The chromium plated collar that threads on to the lower fork leg is difficult to remove without the appropriate Honda service tool - a peg spanner which engages with slots in the periphery of the collar. A strap or a chain spanner can be used as a substitute, provided care is taken to prevent the collar from being distorted as pressure is applied or the chromium plating marked.

4 When the screwed collar is removed, access is available to the circlip within the lower fork leg. When this is withdrawn, the fork stanchion can be pulled out, together with the damper assembly. Note that on some models the spring guide tube is retained by an additional screw deeply recessed into the bottom of the lower fork leg, above the portion normally occupied by the front wheel spindle. The fork spring which is contained within the stanchion tube will also be freed as the stanchion is lifted out.

5 When the snap ring is removed from the bottom of the fork stanchion, the damper piston and limit ring assembly can be drawn off. The fork leg is now dismantled completely; repeat this procedure for the other fork leg.

6 If it is desired to dismantle either or both fork legs without disturbing the steering head races, follow the procedure described in the preceding section, from paragraph 5 to 8 inclusive. Then continue from paragraph 2 of this section, after first removing the bolts from the top of each fork leg. At this stage the forks should be drained of oil.

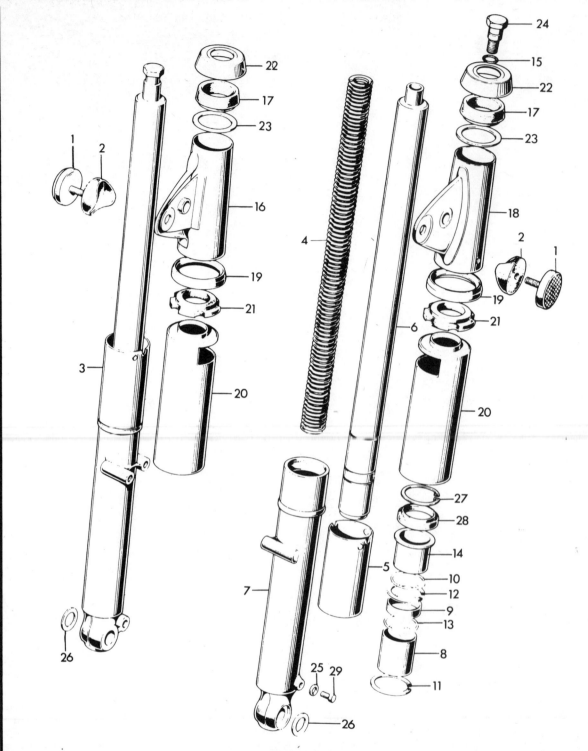

Fig 4.1 FRONT FORKS (CB175/CD175)

1 Reflector - 2 off
2 Reflector base - 2 off
3 Fork leg assembly - 2 off
4 Fork spring - 2 off
5 Bottom fork leg cover - 2 off
6 Fork stanchion - 2 off
7 Lower fork leg - 2 off
8 Damper unit piston - 2 off
9 Damper valve - 2 off
10 Stopper ring - 2 off

11 Piston snap ring - 2 off
12 Valve stopper ring - 2 off
13 Piston limit ring - 2 off
14 Guide bush - 2 off
15 O ring for filler plug - 2 off
16 Upper fork shroud, right hand
17 Upper cushion rubber - 2 off
18 Upper fork shroud - left hand
19 Upper shroud seating - 2 off
20 Lower fork shroud - 2 off

21 Seating for lower fork shroud - 2 off
22 Fork shroud cap - 2 off
23 Washer - 2 off
24 Fork top bolt (filler plug) - 2 off
25 Drain plug washer - 2 off
26 Washer - 2 off
27 Circlip - 2 off
28 Oil seal - 2 off
29 Drain plug - 2 off

4 Steering head bearings - examination and renovation

1 Before commencing reassembly of the forks, examine the steering head races. The ball bearing tracks of the respective cup and cone bearings should be polished and free from indentations and cracks. If signs of wear or damage are evident, the cups and cones must be replaced. They are a tight push fit and should be drifted out of position.

2 Ball bearings are relatively cheap. If the originals are marked or discoloured, they should be replaced without question. To hold the steel balls in position during re-attachment of the forks, pack the bearings with grease. Note that each race should contain a total of nineteen ¼ inch diameter ball bearings. Although space will be left to include one extra ball, it is necessary to prevent the bearings from skidding on each other and accelerating the rate of wear.

5 Front forks - examination and renovation

1 The parts most liable to wear over an extended period of service are the fork bushes and pistons which fit over the fork stanchions and the oil seals below the circlips which retain the fork stanchions within the lower legs of the forks. Worn fork bushes cause judder when the front brake is applied and the increased amount of play can be detected by pulling and pushing on the handlebars when the front brake is applied fully.

2 The fork bushes and the damper pistons are easily replaced since they will be removed during the dismantling operation. This also applies to the oil seals. It is often advisable to renew the various dust seals and seating rubbers on the same occasion, since this will help prolong the life of the oil seals.

3 It is rarely possible to straighten forks which have been badly damaged in an accident, especially if the correct jigs are not available. It is always best to err on the side of safety and fit new replacements, especially since there is no easy means of checking to what extent the forks have been overstressed. The fork stanchions can be checked for straightness by rolling them on a flat surface. Any misalignment will immediately be obvious.

4 The fork springs may show signs of compression after lengthy service, in which case they can be replaced to advantage. They have a free length of 409.3 mm (16.114 in) and should be replaced if the length has reduced to 376 mm (14.803 in) or below.

5 Fork damping is governed by the viscosity of the oil in the fork legs (normally SAE 10W-30) and by the action of the damper piston. The outside diameter of the piston is within the range 35.425 to 35.450 mm (1.3946 to 1.3955 in) but if this falls to 35.400 mm (1.3937 in) as the result of wear, the piston must be replaced. Each fork leg holds from 135 to 145 cc oil.

6 Front forks - replacement

1 Replace the front forks by reversing either of the dismantling procedures described in Sections 2 and 3 of this Chapter, whichever appropriate. Make sure the brake plate is reconnected with the torque arm after the wheel is replaced in the fork ends, otherwise a serious accident may occur when the front brake is applied. On the CD175 model the channel in the brake plate must align with the projection on the left hand fork leg.

2 Before fully tightening the front wheel spindle, fork yoke pinch bolts and the bolts in the top of each fork leg, bounce the forks several times to ensure they work freely and are clamped in their original settings. Complete the final tightening from the wheel spindle upwards.

3 Do not forget to add the recommended quantity of damping oil to each fork leg before the bolts in the top of each fork leg are replaced. Check the drain plugs have been re-inserted and

tightened before the oil is added!

4 Although the fork stanchions are not a taper fit in the top yoke of the forks, difficulty is sometimes experienced when attempting to align the stanchions correctly. It is worth making up a special tool in the form of a threaded rod of the correct diameter and thread to which a 'T' handle is attached. If this is screwed into the top of the stanchion, through the hole in the top yoke, it can be used to draw the stanchion into its correct location.

5 Before the machine is used on the road, check the adjustment of the steering head bearings. If they are too slack, judder will occur. There should be no play at the head races when the handlebars are pulled and pushed, with the front brake fully applied.

6 Overtight head races are equally undesirable. It is possible to unwittingly apply a pressure of several tons on the head bearings by overtightening, even though the handlebars appear to turn quite freely. Overtight bearings will cause the machine to roll at low speeds and give generally imprecise handling. Adjustment is correct if there is no play in the bearings and the handlebars swing to full lock either side when the machine is on the centre stand with the front wheel clear of the ground. Only a light tap on each end should cause the handlebars to swing.

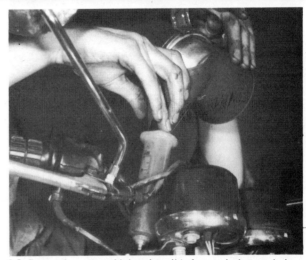

6.3 Do not forget to add damping oil before replacing top bolts

7 Steering head lock

1 The steering head lock is attached to the underside of the lower yoke of the forks by a single screw and washer. When in a locked position, a tongue extends from the body of the lock when the handlebars are on full lock in either direction and abuts against a plate welded to the base of the steering head. In consequence, the handlebars cannot be straightened until the lock is released.

2 If the lock malfunctions, it must be replaced. A repair is impracticable. When the lock is changed the key must be changed too, to match the new lock. No maintenance is necessary; when not in use the lock is protected by a spring-loaded cover plate.

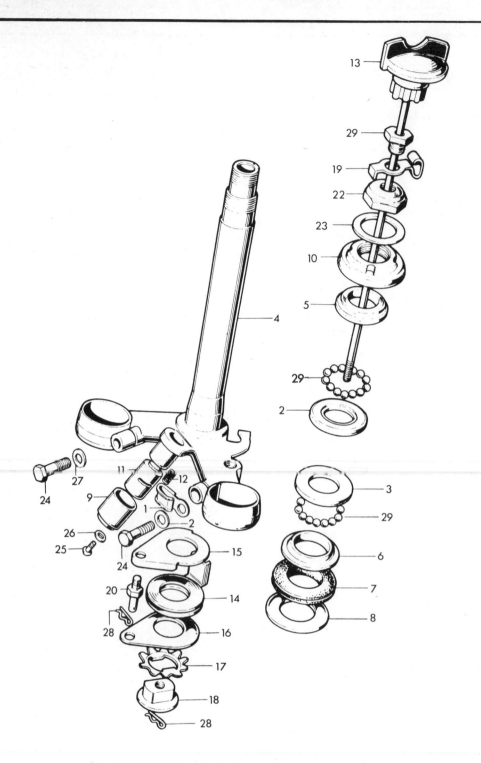

Fig 4.2 STEERING HEAD STEM AND STEERING DAMPER

1 Cable clip
2 Upper steering head cup
3 Lower steering head cup
4 Steering head stem
5 Upper steering head cone
6 Lower steering head cone
7 Dust seal
8 Dust seal washer
9 Cover for steering column lock
10 Steering head adjuster

11 Barrel of steering column lock
12 Lock spring
13 Steering damper knob
14 Steering damper disc
15 Steering damper top plate
16 Steering damper anchor plate
17 Steering damper spring
18 Steering damper nut
19 Steering damper lock spring
20 Friction disc anchor bolt

21 Steering damper lock bolt
22 Steering damper stem nut
23 Stem washer
24 Lower fork yoke pinch bolts
25 Screw for steering column lock
26 Plain washer
27 Pinch bolt washer - 2 off
28 Locking pin - 2 off
29 Ball bearing (¼ inch diameter) - 36 off

8 Steering damper - function and use

1   A steering damper of the friction disc type is fitted to provide a means of adding fraction to the steering head assembly to make the forks turn less easily. It is a relic of the early days of motor cycling when machines were liable to develop 'speed wobbles' without warning. With today's more sophisticated front fork damping and improved frame design, a steering damper is almost a superfluous fitting, except at very high speeds or on poor road surfaces.

2   The steering damper is, in effect, a small clutch without any compression springs. When the steering damper knob is tightened, the friction discs are brought into closer proximity with each other and it is more difficult to deflect the handlebars from their set position. If the knob is tightened fully, the handlebars are virtually in position. Under normal riding conditions the steering damper should be slackened off. Only at very high speeds or on rough surfaces is there need to apply some damper friction.

3   The friction disc assembly will be found at the base of the steering head column, immediately below the bottom fork yoke. The centre fixed plate is attached to the yoke by a screwed peg which forms the left hand lock stop.

4   Although it is unlikely that the steering damper assembly will require attention during the normal service life of the machine, it can be removed by withdrawing the damper knob and rod after the split pin has been withdrawn from the far end. The remainder of the assembly is freed when the left hand lock stop is removed from the bottom yoke of the forks.

9 Frame - examination and renovation

1   The frame is unlikely to require attention unless accident damage has occurred. In some cases, replacement of the frame is the only satisfactory course of action if it is badly out of alignment. Only a few frame repair specialists have the jigs and mandrels necessary for resetting the frame to the required standard of accuracy and even then there is no easy means of assessing to what extent the frame may have been overstressed.

2   After the machine has covered a considerable mileage, it is advisable to examine the frame closely for signs of cracking or splitting at the welded joints. Rust corrosion can also cause weakness at these joints. Minor damage can be repaired by welding or brazing, depending on the extent and nature of the damage.

3   Remember that a frame which is out of alignment will cause handling problems and may even promote 'speed wobbles'. If misalignment is suspected, as the result of an accident, it will be necessary to strip the machine completely so that the frame can be checked and, if necessary, renewed.

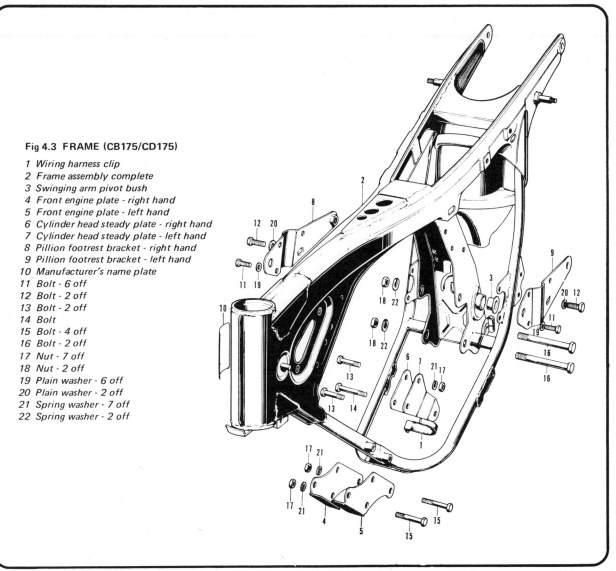

Fig 4.3 FRAME (CB175/CD175)

1 Wiring harness clip
2 Frame assembly complete
3 Swinging arm pivot bush
4 Front engine plate - right hand
5 Front engine plate - left hand
6 Cylinder head steady plate - right hand
7 Cylinder head steady plate - left hand
8 Pillion footrest bracket - right hand
9 Pillion footrest bracket - left hand
10 Manufacturer's name plate
11 Bolt - 6 off
12 Bolt - 2 off
13 Bolt - 2 off
14 Bolt
15 Bolt - 4 off
16 Bolt - 2 off
17 Nut - 7 off
18 Nut - 2 off
19 Plain washer - 6 off
20 Plain washer - 2 off
21 Spring washer - 7 off
22 Spring washer - 2 off

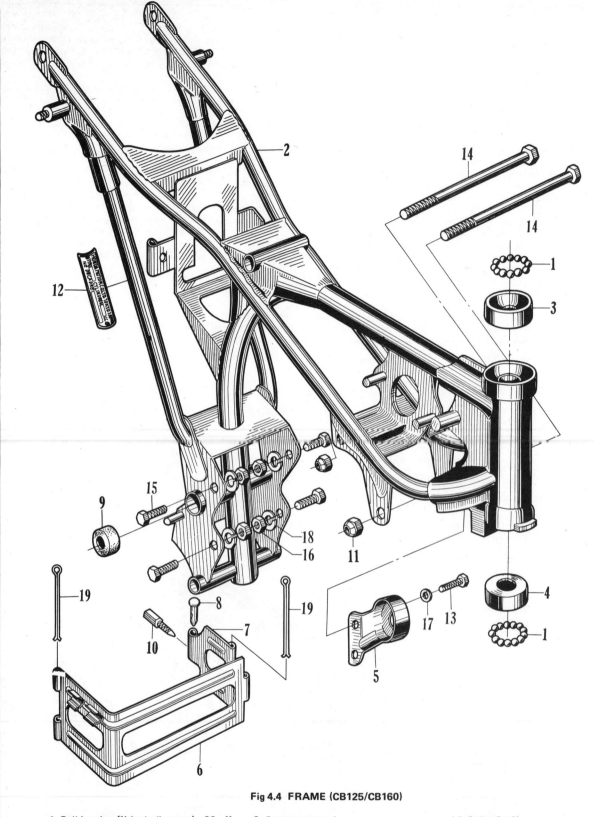

Fig 4.4 FRAME (CB125/CB160)

1 Ball bearing (¼ inch diameter) - 36 off
2 Frame complete
3 Upper steering head cup
4 Lower steering head cup
5 Switch bracket
6 Battery carrier
7 Battery clamp

8 Battery strap pin
9 Rubber dust seal cap - 2 off
10 Battery strap bolt
11 Locknut - 2 off
12 Manufacturer's name plate
13 Bolt

14 Bolt - 2 off
15 Bolt - 4 off
16 Nut - 4 off
17 Flat washer
18 Spring washer - 4 off
19 Split pin - 2 off

10 Swinging arm rear fork - dismantling, examination and renovation

1 The rear fork of the frame assembly pivots on a detachable bush within each end of the fork crossmember and a pivot shaft which passes through the frame lugs and the centre of each of the two bushes. It is quite easy to renovate the swinging arm pivots when wear necessitates attention.

2 To remove the swinging arm fork, first position the machine on its centre stand, then detach the rear chainguard, which is retained by three bolts. (Fully enclosed chainguard, CD175 model.) Two are in a forward position, retaining the front and rear surfaces of the chainguard to lugs welded on the swinging arm fork. The third is at the rear, behind the bottom mounting of the rear suspension unit. Remove the final drive chain at the spring link. Disconnection is made easier if the link is detached whilst the chain ends are pressed into the teeth of the rear wheel sprocket.

3 Detach the rear brake torque arm from the brake plate on the right hand side of the machine by removing the spring clip, then the retaining nut, bolt and washer. Remove the rear brake rod by unscrewing the adjuster from the end and pulling the rod from the trunnion within the brake operating arm. Take care not to lose the trunnion which is now free. Detach the split pin from the left hand end of the rear wheel spindle and unscrew the castellated nut. The wheel spindle can now be withdrawn. Do not misplace the distance piece between the brake plate and the inside of the fork end which will fall clear or the bearing spacer on the sprocket side.

4 Remove the brake plate complete with the rear brake assembly; this will lift away from the wheel. Then remove the rear wheel complete with sprocket by tilting it so that there is sufficient clearance to ease it from under the mudguard and away from the machine.

5 Remove both rear suspension units from the swinging arm fork. Each is bolted at the bottom end to the swinging arm fork, through a rubber bush. The top mounting takes the form of a stud projecting from the subframe which passes through the upper rubber bush mounting of the unit. The unit is secured by an acorn nut which need be slackened only.

6 Remove the rear brake torque arm which is retained by a single bolt at the forward end, then remove the locknut from the end of the fork pivot shaft and withdraw the shaft itself. The swinging arm fork is now free to be withdrawn from the frame.

7 Removal is made easier if the fork is first raised and then pushed forward so that the dust covers can be removed from each end of the pivot housing. They pull off quite easily. Then draw the fork backwards again and tilt the left hand end upwards. It should then clear the frame without difficulty.

8 The two pivot bushes should press out of the ends of the fork crossmember with ease. Wash the bearings and the pivot shaft with a petrol/paraffin mix, then check the amount of play between them. If the clearance exceeds 0.5 mm (0.020 in) the bearings and the pivot shaft should be replaced as a set. If replacement is not necessary, check the pivot shaft for straightness. If it is bent, it must be replaced.

9 Reassemble the swinging arm fork by reversing the dismantling procedure. Grease the pivot shaft and bearings liberally prior to reassembly and check that the seals within the dust covers are in good order.

10 Worn swinging arm pivot bearings will give imprecise handling with a tendency for the rear end of the machine to twitch or hop. The play can be detected by placing the machine on its centre stand and with the rear wheel clear of the ground, pulling and pushing on the fork ends in a horizontal direction. Any play will be greatly magnified by the leverage effect.

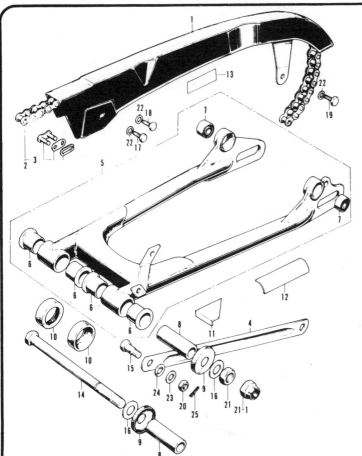

Fig 4.5 SWINGING ARM FORK (CB175/CD175)

1 Rear chainguard
2 Final drive chain
3 Spring link for chain
4 Rear brake torque arm
5 Swinging arm fork complete
6 Bush for swinging arm pivot - 4 off
7 Bush for wear suspension unit - 2 off
8 Bearing - 2 off
9 Dust seal - 2 off
10 Dust seal cap - 2 off
11 Chain slider
12 Silencer caution notice
13 Tyre caution notice
14 Swinging arm pivot bolt
15 Rear brake torque arm bolt
16 Washer
17 Bolt - 2 off
18 Bolt
19 Bolt
20 Nut
21 Nut
22 Washer
23 Plain washer - 2 off
24 Spring washer
25 Split pin

10.2 Rear chainguard is retained by three bolts to swinging arm fork

10.2a Separate rear chain when spring link is in rear wheel sprocket

10.3 Detach spring clip before torque arm bolt is slackened and removed

10.3a Slacken and remove nut from brake rod, to free operating arm

10.3b Withdraw wheel spindle after removing split pin from far end

10.4 Remove brake plate complete from wheel

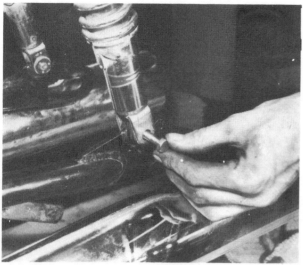

10.5 Rear suspension units are retained by nuts and bolts at lower ends

10.6 Remove the locknut from the pivot shaft ...

10.6a ... then withdraw the pivot shaft itself

10.7 Twist fork to aid removal from frame ...

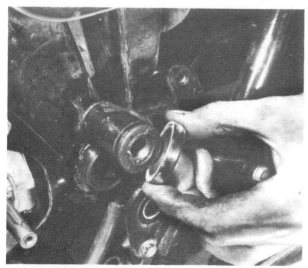

10.7a ... after removing dust covers

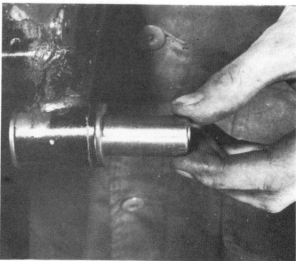

10.8 Bushes press out of each fork end

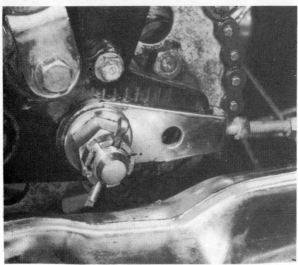

10.9 Do not forget split pin, after tightening rear spindle nut

11 Rear suspension units - examination

1   Rear suspension units of the three-position, hydraulically-damped type are fitted to all the Honda lightweight twins, except the CD175A and CD175K4 models. They can be adjusted to give three different spring settings, in accordance with riding conditions, without need for removal from the machine.
2   Each unit has two peg holes immediately above the adjusting notches to facilitate adjustment. Either a 'C' spanner or a metal rod can be used to turn the adjusters. Rotate clockwise to increase the spring tension and stiffen up the suspension. The recommended settings are as follows:

Position 1 (least tension)   Normal running, without a
                                    pillion passenger
Position 2 (middle position)   High speed touring
Position 3 (most tension)   Very high speed or with pillion
                                    passenger and/or heavy loads

3   There is no means of draining the units or topping up, because the dampers are built as a sealed unit. If the damping fails or if the units commence to leak, the complete damper assembly must be replaced.
4   The compression springs can be removed by detaching the damper units from the machine and holding each one upright on the workbench whilst the outer top shroud is pressed downwards in opposition to the spring pressure. This will permit a second person to remove the split collets from the top of the shroud so that the shroud and spring can be withdrawn over the upper end of the unit. The spring should have a free length of 188.3 mm (7.4133 in) and should be replaced if it has compressed to 174 mm (6.3504 in) or beyond.
5   In the interests of good road holding, it is essential that both units are set to the same load setting and that when replacements are made, both units are treated in an identical manner so that they stay matched.

12 Centre stand - examination

1   The centre stand is attached to the underside of the rear engine plate pressings and pivots on a hollow spindle through which the long retaining bolt passes. An extension spring is used to keep the stand in the fully retracted position whilst the machine is in motion.
2   Check that the return spring is in good condition and that the

pivot bolt is secure. If the stand falls whilst the machine is being ridden, it may catch in some obstacle and unseat the rider.

13 Prop stand - examination

1   A prop stand is also fitted, for use when it is desired not to use the centre stand. The prop stand pivots from a small bracket in the case of the CB125 and CB160 models; a lug on the frame is used in the case of the CB175 and CD175 models. An extension spring ensures the stand is retracted when the weight of the machine is taken off the stand.
2   Check that the pivot bolt is secure and that the extension spring is in good condition and not over-stretched. An accident is almost inevitable if the stand extends whilst the machine is on the move.

14 Footrests - examination and renovation

1   On the CB175 and CD175 models which have a full frame, the footrests bolt as a complete unit to the underside of the lower frame tubes, using tapped lugs. They are not adjustable for height and in the case of the later models, have the footrest arms spring loaded. Early models not having a full frame have a variation of this method of mounting, where the footrest assembly is more rigid throughout.
2   If a machine is dropped, the footrest assembly fitted to the earlier models is likely to suffer the most damage and it will be necessary to remove the footrest bar complete before straightening can be tackled. Never attempt to bend the footrests straight whilst they are still attached to the machine. It is best to remove the assembly complete and straighten it in a vice, preferably using a blow lamp to heat the damaged area to a dull cherry red whilst it is being straightened. It follows that the footrest rubbers must be removed temporarily during this operation to prevent damage from heat conduction.

15 Rear brake pedal - examination and renovation

1   The rear brake pedal pivots around an extension of the centre stand pivot and is held captive by a washer and split pin which passes through the end of the tube. A·coil spring attached to a lug welded on to the brake pedal arm ensures the pedal returns to its normal operating position.
2   If the brake pedal is bent or twisted in an accident, it should be removed and straightened in a manner similar to that recommended for the footrests in the preceding Section.

16 Dual seat - removal and replacement

1   The dual seat is attached to two lugs on the left hand side of the subframe and pivots from these attachments so that it opens from the right. The dual seat locks in position on the CB175K6 models, safeguarding the battery and on some models, helmets can be attached to hooks that are locked individually.
2   If it is necessary to detach the dual seat, remove the split pins through each of the two hinge pins at the pivots and withdraw the hinge pins. The dual seat can now be lifted away as a complete unit.
3   Earlier models have a different arrangement. Two bolts, one on each side of the dual seat, must be removed before the dual seat can be lifted off the machine.

17 Speedometer and tachometer heads - removal and replacement

1 All models, with the exception of the CD175A and CD175K4, have a combined speedometer and tachometer (combined unit, CB160 model). The instrument head is housed within the headlamp shell in a specially raised extension. The CB175 model has both a speedometer and a tachometer in the form of separate instruments. Each is contained within a rubber case, attached to a bracket across the fork tops, secured by the two bolts which act as filler plugs and also retain the top of each fork leg to the top yoke.

2 Before any of the instrument heads can be removed, it is first necessary to detach the drive cable. Unscrew the coupling nut from the underside of each instrument and pull the cables away.

3 The internal bulbs will also pull away from the underside of each instrument head, complete with their rubber-covered bulb holders. They are a push fit onto the base of the instrument.

4 Apart from defects in either the drive or the drive cable, a speedometer or tachometer which malfunctions is difficult to repair. Fit a replacement or alternatively entrust the repair to a competent instrument repair specialist.

5 Remember that a speedometer in correct working order is a statutory requirement in the UK. Apart from this legal necessity, reference to the odometer reading is the most satisfactory means of keeping pace with the maintenance schedules.

6 The combined unit used on the CB160 models is fitted into the headlamp shell.

18 Speedometer and tachometer drive cables - examination and maintenance

1 It is advisable to detach the drive cable(s) from time to time in order to check whether they are lubricated adequately, and whether the outer coverings are damaged or compressed at any point along their run. Jerky or sluggish movements can often be traced to a damaged drive cable.

2 For greasing, withdraw the inner cable. After removing all the old grease, clean with a petrol-soaked rag and examine the cable for broken strands or other damage.

3 Regrease the cable with high melting point grease, taking care not to grease the last six inches at the point where the cable enters the instrument head. If this precaution is not observed, grease will work into the head and immobilise the instrument movement.

4 If any instrument head stops working, suspect a broken drive cable unless the odometer readings continue. Inspection will show whether the inner cable has broken; if so, the inner cable alone can be replaced and re-inserted in the outer casing, after

greasing. Never fit a new inner cable alone if the outer covering is damaged or compressed at any point along its run.

19 Speedometer and tachometer drives - location and examination

1 The speedometer drive gearbox forms part of the front brake plate assembly and is driven internally from the wheel hub. The tongued drive pinion engages with slots formed on the left hand end of the wheel hub. The drive rarely gives trouble; it is pre-packed with grease and should be relubricated when the front wheel bearings receive attention.

2 When fitted the tachometer is driven from the cover at the right hand end of the overhead camshaft. A worm on the end of the camshaft engages at right angles with a small pinion and this transmits the drive via a flexible cable to the tachometer head. It is unlikely that the drive will give trouble during the normal service life of the machine.

20 Cleaning the machine

1 After removing all surface dirt with a rag or sponge which is washed frequently in clean water, the machine should be allowed to dry thoroughly. Application of car polish or wax to the cycle parts will give a good finish, particularly if the machine receives this attention at regular intervals.

2 The plated parts should require only a wipe with a damp rag, but if they are badly corroded, as may occur during the winter when the roads are salted, it is permissible to use one of the proprietary chrome cleaners. These often have an oily base which will help to prevent corrosion from recurring.

3 If the engine parts are particularly oily, use a cleaning compound such as Gunk or Jizer. Apply the compound whilst the parts are dry and work it in with a brush so that it has an opportunity to penetrate and soak into the film of oil and grease. Finish off by washing down liberally, taking care that water does not enter the carburettors, air cleaners or the electrics. If desired, the now clean aluminium alloy parts can be enhanced still further when they are dry by using a special polish such as Solvol Autosol. This will restore the full lustre.

4 If possible, the machine should be wiped down immediately after it has been used in the wet, so that it is not garaged under damp conditions that will promote rusting. Make sure the chain is wiped and re-oiled, to prevent water from entering the rollers and causing harshness with an accompanying rapid rate of wear. Remember there is less chance of water entering the control cables and causing stiffness if they are lubricated regularly as described in the Routine Maintenance section.

21 Fault diagnosis

Symptom	Cause	Remedy
Machine veers to left or right with hands off handlebars	Incorrect wheel alignment Bent forks Twisted frame	Check and re-align. Check and replace. Check and replace.
Machine rolls at low speeds	Overtight steering head bearings	Slacken and re-test.
Machine judders when front brake is applied	Slack steering head bearings	Tighten until all play is taken up.
Machine pitches badly on uneven surfaces	Ineffective fork dampers Ineffective rear suspension units	Check oil content. Check damping action.
Fork action stiff	Fork legs out of alignment (twisted in yokes)	Slacken yoke clamps, front wheel spindle and fork top bolts. Pump forks several times, then tighten from bottom upwards.
Machine wanders. Steering imprecise, rear wheel tends to hop	Worn swinging arm pivot	Dismantle and replace bushes and pivot shaft.

Chapter 5 Wheels, Brakes and Tyres

Contents

Specifications

	CB125	CB160	CB175K4/K6	CD175A/CD175K4
Tyres				
Front	2.50 x 18 in		2.75 x 18 in	2.75 x 17 in
Rear	2.75 x 18 in		3.00 x 18 in	3.00 x 17
Brakes				
Front		7 inch diameter		
Type		Twin leading shoe *		
Rear		7 inch diameter		
Type		Single leading shoe		

   * CD175 model has single leading shoe brake

Tyre pressures	
Front	26 lbs psi
Rear	28 lbs psi

   NOTE: Increase the rear tyre pressure by about 4 lbs psi when a pillion passenger is carried

1 General description

The CB125 and CB160 models have 18 inch diameter wheels. The front tyre is of 2.50 inch section and is normally of the ribbed tread variety. The rear tyre is of 2.75 inch section and has a block tread. The CB175 model has 18 inch diameter wheels, the CD175 models 17 inch. Both front and rear tyres have a ribbed and block tread pattern respectively. All models employ steel wheel rims in conjunction with cast aluminium alloy hubs. Each wheel has, as standard, a 7 inch internal expanding brake which is of the twin leading shoe variety in the case of all models with the exception of the CD175. This latter model has a single leading shoe brake unit.

Both wheels are quickly detachable but it is not possible to remove the rear wheel without having to detach the final drive chain (remove chaincase first CD175 model).

2 Front wheel - examination and renovation

1   Place the machine on the centre stand so that the front wheel is raised clear of the ground. Spin the wheel and check the rim alignment. Small irregularities can be corrected by tightening the spokes in the affected area although a certain amount of experience is necessary to prevent over-correction. Any flats in the wheel rim will be evident at the same time. These are more difficult to remove and in most cases it will be necessary to have the wheel rebuilt on a new rim. Apart from the effect on stability, a flat will expose the tyre bead and walls to greater risk of damage if the machine is run with a deformed wheel.

2   Check for loose and broken spokes. Tapping the spokes is the best guide to tension. A loose spoke will produce a quite different sound and should be tightened by turning the nipple in an anticlockwise direction. Always check for run out by spinning the wheel again. If the spokes have to be tightened by an excessive amount, it is advisable to remove the tyre and tube as detailed in Section 13 of this Chapter. This will enable the protruding ends of the spokes to be ground off, thus preventing them from chafing the inner tube and causing punctures.

3.1 Brake assembly is free when wheel is removed from frame

3.3 Twin leading shoe brake has two separate operating cams

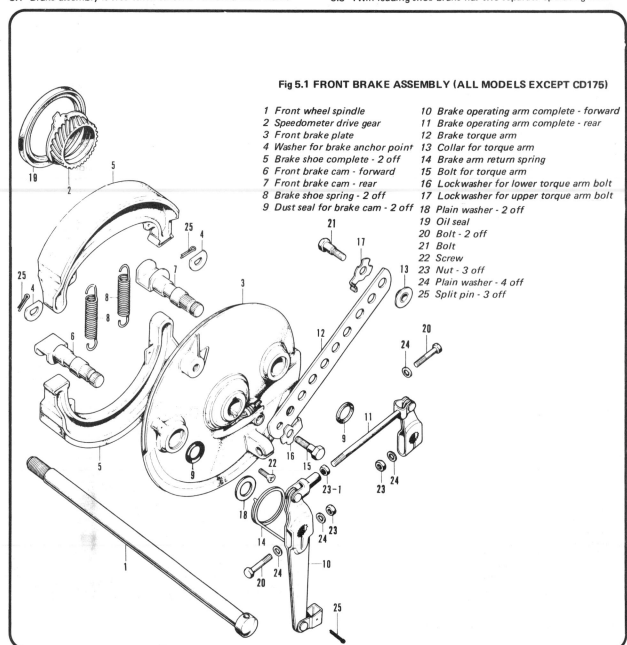

Fig 5.1 FRONT BRAKE ASSEMBLY (ALL MODELS EXCEPT CD175)

1 Front wheel spindle
2 Speedometer drive gear
3 Front brake plate
4 Washer for brake anchor point
5 Brake shoe complete - 2 off
6 Front brake cam - forward
7 Front brake cam - rear
8 Brake shoe spring - 2 off
9 Dust seal for brake cam - 2 off

10 Brake operating arm complete - forward
11 Brake operating arm complete - rear
12 Brake torque arm
13 Collar for torque arm
14 Brake arm return spring
15 Bolt for torque arm
16 Lockwasher for lower torque arm bolt
17 Lockwasher for upper torque arm bolt
18 Plain washer - 2 off
19 Oil seal
20 Bolt - 2 off
21 Bolt
22 Screw
23 Nut - 3 off
24 Plain washer - 4 off
25 Split pin - 3 off

3 Front brake assembly - examination, renovation and reassembly

1 The front brake assembly complete with the brake plate can be withdrawn from the front wheel hub after the wheel spindle has been pulled out and the wheel removed from the fork ends. Refer to Chapter 4, Sections 2.6 and 2.7 for the recommended procedure.

2 Examine the condition of the brake linings. If they are thin or uneven, the brake shoes should be replaced. The linings are bonded on and cannot be supplied separately.

3 To remove the brake shoes, turn the brake operating lever so that the brake is in the fully on position. Pull the brake shoes apart against their return spring pressure to free them from their operating cams, after withdrawing the split pins used to anchor their ends. The shoes can then be lifted away, complete with the return springs by reverting to a 'V' formation. When they are clear of the brake plate, the return springs can be removed and the shoes separated.

4 Before replacing the brake shoes, check that both brake operating cams (single operating cam, CD175 model only) are working smoothly and not binding in their pivot bushes. The cams are removed for greasing by detaching the operating arm from the splined end of each shaft, after first slackening the pinch bolts. Before the arms are pulled off the splines, it is advisable to mark both the operating arm and the shaft to ensure they are replaced in identical positions. Do not alter the setting of the screwed rod which joins both brake operating arms, otherwise the brake will require re-adjustment after assembly.

5 Check the inner surface of the brake drum. The surface on which the brake shoes operate should be smooth and free from score marks or indentations, otherwise reduced braking efficiency will be inevitable. Remove all traces of brake lining dust and wipe with a clean rag soaked in petrol to remove all traces of grease and oil.

6 To reassemble the brake shoes on the brake plate, fit the return springs and pull the shoes apart, holding them in 'V' formation. If they are now located with the brake operating cams and pivots, they can be pushed back into position by pressing downwards in order to snap them into position. Do not use excessive force, or there is risk of distorting the brake shoes permanently.

4 Front wheel bearings - examination and replacement

1 Access is available to the front wheel bearings when the brake plate has been removed. This exposes the left hand wheel bearing; it is protected by an oil seal when the brake plate is in position, the oil seal remaining captive with the brake plate.

2 Lay the wheel brake drum downwards and drive the left hand bearing from the hub using a double-diameter drift which locates with the right hand bearing. When the bearing is displaced, the distance piece which separates the two bearings can also be taken out.

3 Working from the inside of the hub, use the same drift to displace the right hand bearing. The oil seal which precedes the bearing will be displaced at the same time.

4 The CB125 and CB160 models have a distance piece between the two bearings which has shoulders at each end. These aid bearing removal if the correct diameter drift is used. There is also a bearing retainer in front of the left hand bearing which is retained by three screws. This must be removed before the left hand bearing can be displaced from the hub.

5 Remove all the old grease from the hub and bearings, giving the latter a final wash in petrol. Check the bearings for play or any signs of roughness as they are rotated. If there is any doubt about their condition, replace them.

6 Before driving the bearings back into the hub, pack the hub with new grease and also grease the bearings. Use the same double-diameter drift to drive them back into position, not

forgetting the hollow distance piece between them. Refit any oil seals or dust covers which have been displaced and do not omit to replace the bearing retaining plate fitted to the CB125 and CB160 models.

5 Front wheel - reassembly and replacement

1 Place the front brake plate and brake assembly in the brake drum and replace the wheel in the forks. It may be necessary to spring apart the lower ends of the fork legs a little in order to get the wheel to seat correctly. Push the wheel spindle into position and make sure the split pin is located through the right hand end when the spindle is tightened fully.

2 Do not omit to replace and tighten the front brake torque arm. If this should work loose, a serious accident may result because there is nothing to restrain the brake plate from moving in unison with the brake drum.

3 Make sure all wheel nuts and bolts are tight and that the speedometer drive cable is located correctly. Spin the wheel to check that it revolves freely and check that the brake operates correctly, especially if the brake operating arms have been removed during the dismantling sequence. If necessary, re-adjust the brake as described in Section 8 of this Chapter.

6 Rear wheel - examination, removal and renovation

1 Place the machine on the centre stand so that the rear wheel is raised clear of the ground. Check for rim alignment, damage to the rim and loose or broken spokes by following the procedure relating to the front wheel, described in Section 2 of this Chapter.

2 To remove the rear wheel, use the procedure described in Section 10, paragraphs 2 to 4 of Chapter 4. There is however no necessity to detach the chainguard on this occasion.

3 The rear brake plate and brake assembly can be withdrawn from the right hand side of the wheel hub, when the distance piece between the brake plate and the inside of the right hand fork end is removed.

4 The rear wheel bearings are also a drive fit in the hub, separated by a spacer. Use a similar technique for removing, greasing and replacing the bearings to that adopted for the front wheel, as described in Section 4 of this Chapter. Note that the left hand bearing is retained in the hub by a circlip which must be removed after the final drive sprocket is pulled off the cush drive.

6.4 Wheel bearings drive out of hub

6.4a ... are separated by a hollow spacer

6.4b Left hand rear wheel bearing has a retaining circlip, under oil seal

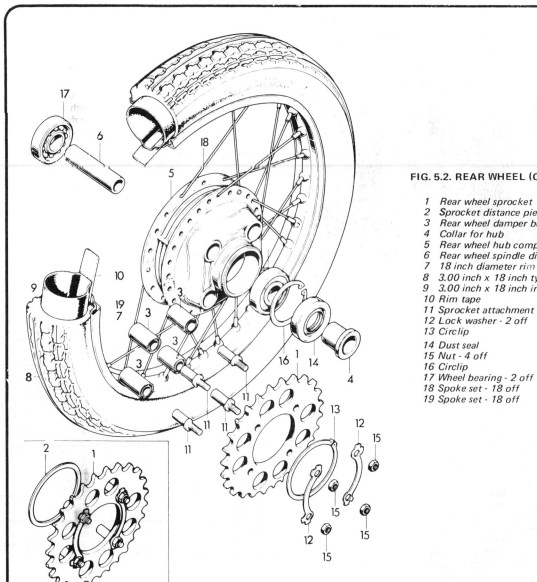

FIG. 5.2. REAR WHEEL (CB175/CD175)

1 Rear wheel sprocket
2 Sprocket distance piece
3 Rear wheel damper bush - 4 off
4 Collar for hub
5 Rear wheel hub complete
6 Rear wheel spindle distance piece
7 18 inch diameter rim
8 3.00 inch x 18 inch tyre
9 3.00 inch x 18 inch inner tube
10 Rim tape
11 Sprocket attachment bolt - 4 off
12 Lock washer - 2 off
13 Circlip
14 Dust seal
15 Nut - 4 off
16 Circlip
17 Wheel bearing - 2 off
18 Spoke set - 18 off
19 Spoke set - 18 off

7 Rear brake assembly - examination, renovation and reassembly

1 The rear brake is of the single leading shoe variety and therefore differs slightly from the front brake, except in the case of the CD175 model, where the brakes are identical.
2 If it is necessary to dismantle the rear brake assembly, follow the procedure given in Section 3 of this Chapter which applies to the front wheel. The same dismantling technique applies to both the single and twin leading shoe designs.

8 Adjusting the twin leading shoe front brake

All models except CD175
1 If the front brake adjustment is correct, there should be a clearance of not less than 20 to 30 mm (0.8 to 1.2 inch) between the brake lever and the handlebars when the brake is applied fully.
2 Adjustment is effected by turning the adjuster nut in the end of the handlebar inwards to decrease the clearance or outwards to

7.1 Rear brake is of single leading shoe type

increase the clearance. If the adjuster on the front brake plate is used, this operates in a similar sequence.
3 The screwed operating rod which links both operating arms of the twin leading shoe front brake should not require adjustment unless the original setting has been disturbed. It is imperative that the leading edge of each brake shoe contacts the brake drum simultaneously if maximum braking efficiency is to be maintained. Check by detaching the clevis pin from the eye of one end of the operating rod so that the brake operating arms can be applied independently. Operate each arm separately and note when the brake shoe first makes contact with the brake drum surface. Make a mark to show the exact position of each operating arm when this initial contact is made. Replace the clevis pin and check that the marks coincide when the brake is applied in similar fashion. If they do not, withdraw the clevis pin and use the adjuster to either extend or reduce the length of the connecting rod until the marks correspond exactly. Replace the clevis pin and do not omit to insert the split pin through the end which retains the clevis pin in position. Recheck the brake lever adjustment before taking the machine on the road.
4 As a rough guide, the two brake operating arms should be parallel to one another when adjustment is correct.
5 Check that the brake pulls off correctly when the handlebar lever is released. Sluggish action is usually due to a poorly

lubricated control cable, broken or extended brake shoe return springs, or a tendency for the brake operating cams to bind in their bushes. Binding brakes affect engine performance and can cause severe overheating of both the brake shoes and the wheel bearings.

CD175 model only
6 Since this model has only a single leading shoe front brake, only two forms of adjustment are available, at the handlebar lever and at the front brake plate. Adjustment is effected as described in paragraph 2.

9 Adjusting the rear brake

1 If the adjustment of the rear brake is correct, the brake pedal will have a travel of from 20 to 30 mm (0.8 to 1.2 inch). Adjustment is made at the end of the brake operating rod, at the point where the rod passes through the trunnion in the brake operating arm. To decrease pedal movement, screw the adjusting nut inwards and vice versa.
2 Note that it may be necessary to re-adjust the height of the stop lamp switch if the range of pedal travel has been altered to any marked extent.

10 Cush drive assembly - examination and renovation

1 The cush drive assembly is contained in the left hand side of the rear wheel hub. It takes the form of four circular rubber bushes inserted into the hub which engage with a pegged plate to which the final drive sprocket is bolted. The drive is transmitted via these rubber, which permit the sprocket to move within certain limits and cushion any surges or roughness in the transmission which would otherwise convey the impression of harshness.
2 When the rear wheel is removed from the machine, remove the circlip around the hub and pull the sprocket from the cush drive assembly. Examine the rubbers for signs of damage or general deterioration. Replace the rubbers if there is any doubt about their condition. The usual sign of the cush drive assembly requiring attention takes the form of excessive sprocket movement.

10.1 Rubbers in hub periphery provide cush drive for sprocket

10.1a Studs on sprocket engage with rubbers

11.1 Circlip must be removed before sprocket can be withdrawn from hub

11.1a Pegs bolt to sprocket. Note distance piece in centre of hub

11 Rear wheel sprocket - removal, examination and replacement

1 The rear wheel sprocket is retained to the hub of the rear wheel by a circlip around the outer periphery of the hub. When this is removed, the sprocket can be pulled from the cush drive assembly; it is bolted to four pegs which engage with the circular rubber bushes within the cush drive assembly. The CD175 model has a variation of this arrangement which incorporates a dust seal for the fully-enclosed final drive chain.

2 It should not be necessary to remove the four nuts and tab washers retaining the rear wheel sprocket to the cush drive pegs unless the teeth are chipped, broken or hooked, necessitating replacement.

3 It is considered bad practice to renew one sprocket on its own. The final drive sprockets should always be renewed as a pair and a new chain fitted, otherwise rapid wear will necessitate even earlier replacement on the next occasion.

4 No advantage is gained from varying the size of either sprocket. The sizes selected have been chosen by the manufacturer as the result of exhaustive tests, to give optimum performance with the existing engine characteristics.

12 Final drive chain - examination and lubrication

1 The final drive chain is fully exposed, except in the case of the CD175 model, where it is enclosed within a full chaincase. In this latter instance, the chaincase affords only a means of protection from grit and other foreign matter; it does not contain any lubricant.

2 Irrespective of the amount of protection provided, the chain tension will need adjustment at regular intervals, to compensate for wear. This is accomplished by slackening the rear wheel nut, after withdrawing the split pin, when the machine is on the centre stand. The draw bolt adjusters in each rear fork end are used to draw the wheel backwards until the chain is again under correct tension. Note that it may be necessary to slacken the rear brake torque arm bolt during this operation.

3 Chain tension is correct if there is from 15 to 20 mm (0.6 to 0.8 inch) of slack in the middle of the upper arm. The CD175 model has a rubber plug in the upper portion of the chaincase to facilitate inspection. Always check the chain at its tightest point; a chain rarely wears in an even manner during service.

4 Always adjust the draw bolts an even amount so that correct wheel alignment is preserved. The fork ends are marked with a series of vertical lines to provide a visual check. If desired, wheel alignment can be checked by running a plank of wood parallel to the machine so that it touches both walls of the rear tyre. If wheel alignment is correct, it should be equidistant from either side of the front wheel tyre when tested on both sides of the rear wheel. Except in the case of the CB175 and CD175 models where the front and rear tyre sizes are identical, it will not touch the front tyre because this tyre has a smaller cross section. See the accompanying diagram.

5 Do not run the chain overtight to compensate for uneven wear. A tight chain will place excessive stresses on the gearbox and rear wheel bearings leading to their early failure. It will also absorb a surprising amount of power.

6 After a period of running, the chain will require lubrication. Lack of oil will accelerate the rate of wear of both chain and sprockets and will lead to harsh transmission. The application of engine oil will act as a temporary expedient, but it is preferable to remove the chain and immerse it in a molten lubricant such as Linklyfe or Chainguard after it has been cleaned in a paraffin bath. These latter lubricants achieve better penetration of the chain links and rollers and are less likely to be thrown off when the chain is in motion.

7 To check whether the chain is due for replacement, lay it lengthwise in a straight line and compress it endwise until all play is taken up. Anchor one end, then pull in the opposite

direction to take up the play which develops. If the chain extends by more than ¼ inch per foot, it should be replaced in conjunction with the sprockets. Note that this check should ALWAYS be made after the chain has been washed out, but before any lubricant is applied, otherwise the lubricant may take up some of the play.

8 When replacing the chain on the machine, make sure the spring link is positioned correctly with the closed end facing the direction of travel.

12.4 Fork ends are marked to aid alignment of chain adjusters

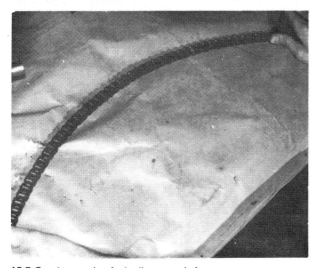

12.7 Good example of a badly worn chain

13 Tyres - removal and replacement

1 At some time or other the need will arise to remove and replace the tyres, either as the result of a puncture or because a replacement is required to offset wear. To the inexperienced, tyre changing represents a formidable task yet if a few simple rules are observed and the technique learned, the whole operation is surprisingly simple.

2 To remove the tyre from either wheel, first detach the wheel from the machine by following the procedure in Chapters 4.2, paragraphs 5 to 7 or 4.10, paragraphs 2 to 4, depending on whether the front or the rear wheel is involved. Deflate the tyre by removing the valve insert and when it is fully deflated, push the bead of the tyre away from the wheel rim on both sides so

that the bead enters the centre well of the rim. Remove the locking cap and push the tyre valve into the tyre itself.

3 Insert a tyre lever close to the valve and lever the edge of the tyre over the outside of the wheel rim. Very little force should be necessary; if resistance is encountered it is probably due to the fact that the tyre beads have not entered the well of the wheel rim all the way round the tyre.

4 Once the tyre has been edged over the wheel rim, it is easy to work around the wheel rim so that the tyre is completely free on one side. At this stage, the inner tube can be removed.

5 Working from the other side of the wheel, ease the other edge of the tyre over the outside of the wheel rim that is furthest away. Continue to work around the rim until the tyre is free completely from the rim.

6 If a puncture has necessitated the removal of the tyre, re-inflate the inner tube and immerse it in a bowl of water to trace the source of the leak. Mark its position and deflate the tube. Dry the tube and clean the area around the puncture with a petrol soaked rag. When the surface has dried, apply the rubber solution and allow this to dry before removing the backing from the patch and applying the patch to the surface.

7 It is best to use a patch of the self-vulcanising type which will form a very permanent repair. Note that it may be necessary to remove a protective covering from the top surface of the patch, after it has sealed in position. Inner tubes made from synthetic rubber may require a special type of patch and adhesive if a satisfactory bond is to be achieved.

8 Before replacing the tyre, check the inside to make sure the agent which caused the puncture is not trapped. Check also the outside of the tyre, particularly the tread area, to make sure nothing is trapped that may cause a further puncture.

9 If the inner tube has been patched on a number of past occasions, or if there is a tear or large hole, it is preferable to discard it and fit a replacement. Sudden deflation may cause an accident, particularly if it occurs with the front wheel.

10 To replace the tyre, inflate the inner tube sufficiently for it to assume a circular shape but only just. Then push it into the tyre so that it is enclosed completely. Lay the tyre on the wheel at an angle and insert the valve captive in its correct location.

11 Starting at the point furthest from the valve, push the tyre bead over the edge of the wheel rim until it is located in the central well. Continue to work around the tyre in this fashion until the whole of one side of the tyre is on the rim. It may be necessary to use a tyre lever during the final stages.

12 Make sure there is no pull on the tyre valve and again commencing with the area furthest from the valve, ease the other bead of the tyre over the edge of the rim. Finish with the area close to the valve, pushing the valve up into the tyre until the locking cap touches the rim. This will ensure the inner tube is not trapped when the last section of the bead is edged over the rim with a tyre lever.

13 Check that the inner tube is not trapped at any point. Re-inflate the inner tube, and check that the tyre is seating correctly around the wheel rim. There should be a thin rib moulded around the wall of the tyre on both sides which should be equidistant from the wheel rim at all points. If the tyre is unevenly located on the rim, try bouncing the wheel when the tyre is at the recommended pressure. It is probable that one of the beads has not pulled clear of the centre well.

14 Always run the tyres at the recommended pressures and never under or over-inflate. The correct pressures for solo use are given in the Specifications section of this Chapter. If a pillion passenger is carried, increase the rear tyre pressure only by approximately 4 psi.

15 Tyre replacement is aided by dusting the side walls, particularly in the vicinity of the beads, with a liberal coating of French chalk. Washing up liquid can also be used to good effect, but this has the disadvantage of causing the inner surfaces of the wheel rim to rust.

16 Never replace the inner tube and tyre without the rim tape in position. If this precaution is overlooked there is good chance of the ends of the spoke nipples chafing the inner tube and causing a crop of punctures.

17 Never fit a tyre which has a damaged tread or side walls. Apart from the legal aspects, there is a very great risk of a blow-out which can have serious consequences on any two-wheel vehicle.

18 Tyre valves rarely give trouble, but it is always advisable to check whether the valve itself is leaking before removing the tyre. Do not forget to fit the dust cap, which forms an effective second seal.

14 Fault diagnosis

Symptom	Cause	Remedy
Handlebars oscillate at low speeds	Buckle or flat in wheel rim, most probably front wheel	Check rim alignment by spinning wheel. Correct by retensioning spokes or having wheel rebuilt on new rim.
	Tyre not straight on rim	Check tyre alignment.
Machine lacks power and accelerates poorly	Brakes binding	Warm brake drums provide best evidence. Re-adjust brakes.
Brakes grab when applied gently	Ends of brake shoes not chamfered	Chamfer with file.
	Elliptical brake drum	Lightly skim in lathe (specialist attention needed).
Brake pull-off sluggish	Brake cam binding in housing	Free and grease.
	Weak brake shoe springs	Replace, if brake springs not displaced.
Harsh transmission	Worn or badly adjusted chains	Adjust or replace as necessary.
	Hooked or badly worn sprockets	Replace as a pair, together with chain.

Tyre removal: Deflate inner tube and insert lever in close proximity to tyre valve

Use two levers to work bead over the edge of rim

When first bead is clear, remove tyre as shown

Tyre fitting: Inflate inner tube and insert in tyre

Lay tyre on rim and feed valve through hole in rim

Work first bead over rim, using lever in final section

Use similar technique for second bead, finish at tyre valve position

Push valve and tube up into tyre when fitting final section, to avoid trapping

Chapter 6 Electrical System

Contents

Specifications

	CB125	CB160	CB175	CD175
Battery				
Make			Yuasa	Yuasa
Type			MBW3-12E *	—
Voltage			12 volts	6 volts
Amp/hour capacity			9 *	12
Earth			Negative	Negative

* CD175 uses Type B54-6, 12 amp/hr capacity - 6 volt

Generator
Make   ... ... Kokusan EG 19, Denso 37000-024 or Hitachie K107
Output   ... ... 70 watts

Ignition coil
Make   ... ... Kokusan SR 208, Denso 29700-097 or Hitachi CM12

Starter *
Make   ... ... Kokusan CC03, Denso 28000-111 or Hitachi S106
Brush length ... ... 11 - 12.5 mm (0.4330 - 0.4925 in)
Minimum length ... ... 5 mm (0.2 in)

Bulbs
Headlamp 35/35W
Tail/stop lamp   ... ... 7/23W, offset pins
Pilot lamp 4W
Instrument lamps 3W
Indicator lamps 3W
Flashing indicator lamps   ... ... 25W (18W - CD175 models)

All bulbs rated 12 volts except CD175 (6 volt)

NOTE: Some variation in the wattage ratings may occur if the country or state into which the machine is
    exported has different statutory requirements

* Not fitted to CD175 models imported into UK

1 General description

The Honda twin cylinder lightweight models covered by this manual are all fitted with a 12 volt electrical system. The system comprises a crankshaft driven AC generator of the rotating magnet type, surrounded by a stator assembly having six coils. During daytime running only two coils are used because the electrical demand is solely from the ignition circuit and the occasional use of the stop lamp, flashing indicators or horn. At night all six coils are used to meet the heavier demand arising from the use of the lighting equipment.

The output from the generator is AC hence a selenium rectifier is included in the circuit to convert this current to DC so that it can be used to charge the battery. The daytime charging rate is approximately 1.8 amps; at night the charge rate decreases under the full lighting load to just below 1 amp.

The CD175 model has a similar electrical system, operating at only 6 volts.

2 Crankshaft alternator - checking the output

1   As explained in Chapter 3.2, the output from the alternator can be checked by connecting both a voltmeter and an ammeter into the battery circuit. Refer to this Chapter for full details.
2   Note that the test described gives only an approximate indication of whether the alternator is functioning correctly within its prescribed limits. It will be necessary to seek the assistance of either a Honda agent or an auto-electrical expert to determine whether the generator is working at peak efficiency.

3 Battery - examination and maintenance

1   A Yuasa MBW3-12E 12 volt, 9 amp/hour battery is fitted to all models with the exception of the CD175. This latter model has a 6 volt electrical system using a 12 amp/hr capacity battery.
2   The transparent plastics case of the battery permits the upper and lower levels of the electrolyte to be observed by merely raising the battery from its housing under the dual seat or removing the right hand side cover, CD175 model. Maintenance is normally limited to keeping the electrolyte level between the prescribed upper and lower limits and making sure the vent tube is not blocked. The lead plates and their separators are visible through the transparent case, a further guide to the general condition of the battery.
3   Unless acid is spilt, as may occur if the machine falls over, the electrolyte should always be topped up with distilled water to restore the correct level. If acid is spilt onto any part of the machine, it should be neutralised with an alkali such as washing soda or baking powder and washed away with plenty of water, otherwise serious corrosion will occur. Top up with sulphuric acid of the correct specific gravity (1.260 to 1.280) only when spillage has occurred. Check that the vent pipe is well clear of the frame or any of the other cycle parts.
4   It is seldom practicable to repair a cracked battery case because the acid present in the joint will prevent the formation of an effective seal. It is always best to replace a cracked battery, especially in view of the corrosion which will be caused if the acid continues to leak.
5   If the machine is not used for a period, it is advisable to remove the battery and give it a 'refresher' charge every six weeks or so from a battery charger. If the battery is permitted to discharge completely, the plates will sulphate and render the battery useless.

4 Battery - charging procedure

The normal charging rate for the 9 or 12 amp/hour batteries is 1 ampere. A more rapid charge can be given in an emergency but this should be avoided if at all possible because it will shorten the useful working life of the battery.

3.2 Electrolyte level is clearly marked on battery case

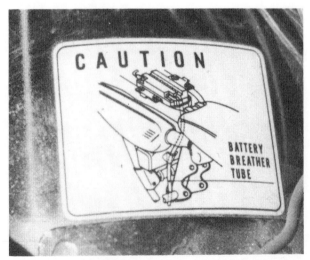

3.3 Vent pipe warning on rear mudguard is self-explanatory

5 Selenium rectifier - general description

1 The function of the selenium rectifier is to convert the AC current produced by the alternator into DC so that it can be used to charge the battery. The rectifier fitted to all models is of the four plate selenium type.

2 The rectifier is located to the rear of the battery, beneath the dual seat, a location where it is afforded reasonable protection. The question of access is of relatively little importance because the rectifier is unlikely to give trouble during normal service. Should it malfunction, a repair is not practicable. It must be replaced.

3 Damage to the rectifier will occur if the machine is run without a battery for any period of time, or with one that no longer holds its charge. A high voltage will develop in the absence of any load across the coils of the alternator which will cause a reverse flow of current and subsequent damage to the rectifier cells. Reverse connection of the battery will have a similar undesirable effect.

4 There is no simple means of checking whether the rectifier is functioning correctly without the appropriate test equipment. A Honda agent or an auto-electrical expert are best qualified to advise, particularly if the battery is in a low state of charge.

5 Do not disturb the rectifier retaining nut or in any way damage the surfaces of the assembly. Any such action may cause the coating over the electrodes to peel or flake and destroy the working action.

6 Fuse - location and replacement

1 A fuse within a moulded plastics case is incorporated in the electrical system to give protection from a sudden overload, such as may occur during a short circuit. It is found in close proximity to the battery, retained in metal clips. The fuse is rated at 15 amps; a plastic bag containing a spare fuse of similar rating is normally carried in a plastics bag attached to the wiring harness.

2 If a fuse blows, it should not be replaced until a check has shown whether a short circuit has occurred. This will involve checking the electrical circuit to identify and correct the fault. If this precaution is not observed, the replacement fuse, which may be the only spare, may blow immediately on connection.

3 When a fuse blows whilst the machine is running and no spare is available, a 'get you home' remedy is to remove the blown fuse and wrap it in silver paper before replacing it in the fuse holder.

The silver paper will restore electrical continuity by bridging the broken wire within the fuse. This expedient should never be used if there is evidence of a short circuit or other major electrical fault, otherwise more serious damage will be caused. Replace the 'doctored' fuse at the earliest possible opportunity to restore full circuit protection.

7 Starter motor - removal, examination and replacement

Not fitted to UK imported CD175 models

1 An electric starter motor, operated from a small push button on the right hand side of the handlebars, provides an alternative means of starting the engine without using the kickstarter. The starter motor is mounted in front of the engine unit, bolted direct to the upper crankcase. Current is supplied from the battery via a heavy duty starter switch and a cable capable of carrying up to 120 amps, the maximum load demanded by the starter motor.

2 The starter motor drives a free running clutch immediately behind the generator rotor. The clutch ensures the starter motor drive is disconnected from the primary transmission immediately the engine starts. It operates on the centrifugal principle; spring loaded rollers take up the drive until the centrifugal force of the rotating engine overcomes their resistance and the drive is automatically disconnected.

3 To remove the starter motor from the engine unit, first disconnect the positive lead from the battery, then the starter motor cable from the terminal on the body of the starter motor itself. If the two cross head screws retaining the starter motor to the upper crankcase are removed, it is ready for withdrawal from the drive assembly.

4 Remove the nine cross head screws which retain the left hand crankcase cover in position and pull the cover away, complete with the stator coil assembly and wiring harness still attached. The starter motor drive is now exposed.

5 The starter motor boss is a tight fit where it enters the extension of the crankcase and it may be necessary to give a few light taps with a rawhide mallet to ease it back. The pinion on the end of the starter motor is splined into position and has no retainer. It should pull off with ease as the starter motor is withdrawn. If the chain is tight, withdraw the spring link first so that the chain can be separated. If the chain is endless, it may be necessary (in extreme cases) to withdraw the starter motor sprocket and the free running clutch sprocket together which will necessitate withdrawing the generator rotor first. Avoid heavy blows on the end of the starter motor spindle at all costs

6.1 Fuse is contained within hinged plastic moulding, which ...

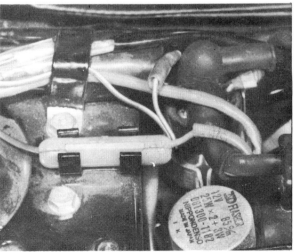

6.1a ... is retained by two metal clips

since this may cause irreparable damage.

6 The only part of the starter motor liable to give trouble is the brushes. If the two long external screws on the outside of the starter motor body are removed, the right hand end cover can be removed, which will expose the commutator and brush gear. Lift up the spring clips which bear on each brush and lift the brushes from their holders. New brushes have a length of 11 to 12.5 mm (0.4330 to 0.4925 inch). The serviceable limit is reached at 5 mm (0.2 inch) when replacement is necessary.

7 Before replacing the brushes, make sure the commutator is clean. Clean with a strip of fine emery cloth pressed against the commutator whilst it is revolved by hand, then wipe with a rag soaked in petrol to ensure a bright, grease-free surface is obtained.

8 Reassemble by reversing the dismantling procedure. If the spring link has been removed from the timing chain, check that it is replaced so that the closed end of the chain faces the direction of travel.

8 Starter motor free running clutch - construction and renovation

Not fitted to UK imported CD175 models

1 Although a mechanical and not an electrical component, it is appropriate to include the free running clutch in this Chapter because it is an essential part of the electric starter system.

2 The free running clutch is built in to the alternator rotor and will be found in the back of the rotor when the latter is removed from the crankshaft. The only parts likely to require attention are the rollers and their springs, or the bush in the centre of the driven sprocket. Access to the rollers is gained by removing the three countersunk screws which hold the clutch body to the rear of the alternator rotor. Signs of wear or damage will be obvious and will necessitate replacements.

3 The bush in the centre of the driven sprocket behind the clutch will need replacing only after very extensive service.

4 To check whether the clutch is operating correctly, turn the driven sprocket anticlockwise. This should force the spring loaded rollers against the crankshaft and cause it to tighten on the crankshaft as the drive is taken up.

9 Starter motor switch - function and location

Not fitted to UK imported CD175 models

1 The starter motor switch is designed to work on the electro-magnetic principle. When the starter motor button is depressed, current from the battery passes through windings in the switch solenoid and generate an electro-magnetic force which causes a set of contact points to close. Immediately the points close, the starter motor is energised and a very heavy current is drawn from the battery.

2 This arrangement is used for at least two reasons. Firstly, the starter motor current is drawn only when the button is depressed and is cut off again when pressure on the button is eased. This ensures minimum drainage on the battery. Secondly, if the battery is in a low state of charge, there will not be sufficient current to cause the solenoid contacts to close. In consequence, it is not possible to place an excessive drain on the battery which, in some circumstances, can cause the plates to overheat and shed their coatings. If the starter will not operate, first suspect a discharged battery. This can be checked by trying the horn or switching on the lights. If this check shows the battery to be in good shape, suspect the starter switch which should come into action with a pronounced click. It is located under the dual seat, close to the battery, and can be identified by the heavy duty starter cable connected to it. It is not possible to effect a satisfactory repair if the switch malfunctions; it must be replaced.

10 Headlamp - replacing bulbs and adjusting beam height

1 In order to gain access to the headlamp bulbs it is necessary first to remove the rim, complete with the reflector and headlamp glass. The rim is retained by two crosshead screws, in the four

and eight o'clock positions when viewed from the front. Remove the screws completely and draw the rim from the headlamp shell.

2 The main headlamp bulb is a push fit into the central bulb holder of the reflector. The bulb holder can be replaced in only one position to ensure the bulb is always correctly focussed; it is retained by a spring under tension. The bulb itself has a flange fitting and is of the pre-focus type. It is of the twin filament type and has a 35/35W rating.

3 The pilot lamp bulb is of the bayonet fitting type and fits within a bulb holder which has the same form of connection to the headlamp reflector. This bulb has a 4W rating.

4 Beam height is adjusted by slackening the two headlamp shell retaining bolts and tilting the headlamp either upwards or downwards. Adjustments should always be made with the rider normally seated. On CD175 models the headlamp shell is fixed. There is a special adjuster screw below the headlamp rim.

5 UK lighting regulations stipulate that the lighting system must be arranged so that the light will not dazzle a person standing in the same horizontal plane as the vehicle at a distance greater than 25 yards from the lamp, whose eye level is not less than 3 feet 6 inches above that plane. It is easy to approximate this setting by placing the machine 25 yards away from a wall, on a level road, and setting the beam height so that it is concentrated at the same height as the distance from the centre of the headlamp to the ground. The rider must be seated normally during this operation and also the pillion passenger, if one is carried regularly.

10.1 Remove screw to release rim and reflector unit

10.2 Main bulb is push fit in reflector unit, retained by spring

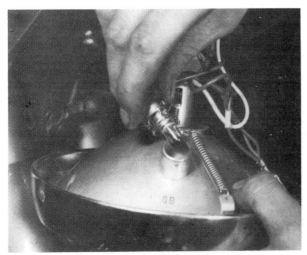

10.3 Pilot bulb has bayonet fitting in reflector unit

11.2 Remove lens cover for access to tail/stop lamp bulb

12.2 Remove lens cover for access to each of the flashing indicator lamps

11 Stop and tail lamp - replacing bulbs

1 The tail lamp has a twin filament bulb of 7/23W rating, to illuminate the rear number plate and to indicate when the rear brake is applied. On some models the stop lamp also operates in conjunction with the front brake; a stop lamp switch is incorporated in the front brake cable to meet the statutory requirements of the country or state to which the machine is exported.

2 To gain access to the stop and tail lamp bulb, unscrew the two crosshead screws which retain the plastics lens cover in position. The bulb has a bayonet fitting and also offset pins so that the stop lamp filament cannot be inadvertently connected with the tail lamp and vice versa.

12 Flashing indicator lamps - replacing bulbs

1 Flashing indicator lamps are fitted to the front and rear of the CB175 and CD175 models. They are mounted on short 'staiks' through which the electrical leads pass. One set of indicators is attached to either side of the fork lug to which the headlamp is attached. The other set are attached to the rear mudguard, immediately beneath the end of the dual seat.

2 Each flasher unit has a bayonet fitting 25W bulb (18W CD175 models). To replace a bulb remove the plastics end cover which is retained by two crosshead screws.

13 Flashing indicator relay - location and replacement

1 The flashing indicator relay fitted in conjunction with the flashing indicator lamps of the CB175 and CD175 models are located with the other electrical components, in the compartment under the dual seat or behind the right hand side cover, CD175 models. It is rubber mounted to isolate it from the harmful effects of vibration.

2 When the relay malfunctions it must be replaced; a repair is impracticable. When the unit is in working order, audible clicks will be heard which keep pace with the flash of the indicator lamps. If the lamps malfunction, check firstly that a bulb failure is not responsible, or the handlebar switch faulty. The usual symptom of a fault is one initial flash before the unit goes dead.

3 Take great care when handling a flashing indicator relay. It is easily damaged, if dropped.

14 Speedometer head - replacement of bulbs

Irrespective of the type of speedometer head fitted, it contains three indicator bulbs and also a bulb for illuminating the dial when the lights are used. The three indicator bulbs show when neutral is selected (green), when the headlamp is on main beam (red) and when the flashing indicators are being used (yellow). Each of the bulbs has a bayonet fitting and is rated at 3W. The bulb holders push into the base of the speedometer head and are secured by their rubber mountings.

15 Horn - adjustment

1 The horn is provided with an adjusting screw in the back of the horn body so that the sound volume can be varied, if necessary. To adjust the horn note, turn the screw not more than one half turn in either direction and test. If the note is weaker, or lost altogether, turn in the opposite direction. Continue adjusting by one half turn at a time until the desired volume and note is obtained.

2 The horn button is located on the left hand side of the handlebars. If the horn does not operate and an electrical meter shows no current is passing through the horn when the horn button is depressed, check the continuity of the light green coloured wire within the headlamp shell.

15.2 Horn button and other electrical connections are made within headlamp shell

16 Handlebar switches - general

1 The arrangement of the handlebar switches will depend on the model concerned. Generally speaking, the switches give little trouble, but if necessary, they can be dismantled by separating the halves which form a split clamp around the handlebars.

2 Always disconnect the battery before removing any of the switches to prevent the possibility of a short circuit. Most troubles are caused by dirty contacts; in the event of breakage of some internal part it will be necessary to replace the complete switch.

17 Ignition and lighting switch - removal and replacement

1 The main switch which controls both the ignition system and the lighting is attached to a bracket on the left hand side of the machine with its back facing the back of the horn. The bracket bolts to the gusset immediately behind the steering head.

2 If the switch proves defective, it can be removed by unscrewing the two bolts which secure the bracket to the frame and separating the terminal connector at the end of the short wiring harness. To release the switch unit itself, unscrew the threaded ring around the outside of the lock.

3 Fit the new switch through the bracket, tighten the threaded ring, then bolt the switch bracket to the frame gusset. Reconnect the wires at the terminal connector. Remember that when a new switch is fitted, it will be necessary also to change the ignition key, and usually, the front fork lock, as a set.

18 Stop lamp switches - adjustment

1 All models have a stop lamp switch fitted to operate in conjunction with the rear brake pedal. The switch is located immediately to the rear of the crankcase, on the right hand side of the machine. It has a threaded body, permitting a range of adjustment.

2 If the stop lamp is late in operating, slacken the locknuts and turn the body of the lamp in an anticlockwise direction so that the switch rises from the bracket to which it is attached. When the adjustment seems near correct, tighten the locknuts and test.

3 If the lamp operates too early, the locknuts should be slackened and the switch body turned clockwise so that it is lowered in relation to the mounting bracket.

4 As a guide, the light should operate after the brake pedal has been depressed by about 2 cm (¾ inch).

5 Some models have a stop lamp switch incorporated in the front brake cable, to give warning when the front brake is applied. This is not yet a statutory requirement in the UK, although it applies in many other countries and states.

6 The front stop lamp switch is built into the front brake cable, but contains provision for adjustment in the form of an in-line cable adjuster. The stop lamp should operate when the front brake lever has been depressed by about 2 cm (¾ inch).

19 Fault diagnosis

Symptom	Cause	Remedy
Complete electrical failure	Blown fuse	Check wiring and electrical components for short circuit before fitting new 15 amp fuse.
	Isolated battery	Check battery connections, also whether connections show signs of corrosion.
Dim lights, horn and starter inoperative	Discharged battery	Recharge battery with battery charger. Check whether generator is giving correct output.
Constantly blowing bulbs	Vibration, poor earth connection	Check security of bulb holders. Check earth return connections.
Starter motor sluggish	Worn brushes	Remove end cover and replace worn brushes.

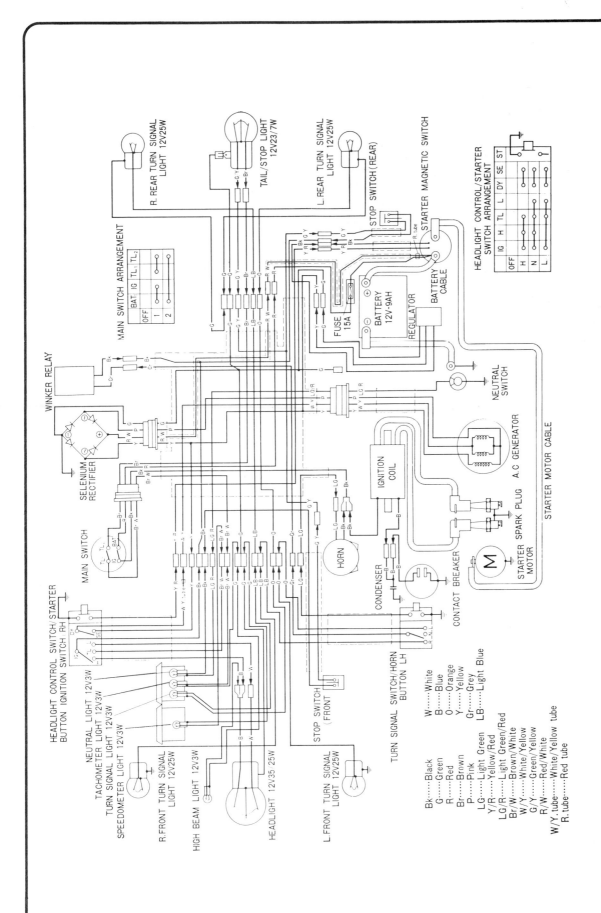

Fig 6.1 WIRING DIAGRAM:·CB175 - USA TYPE

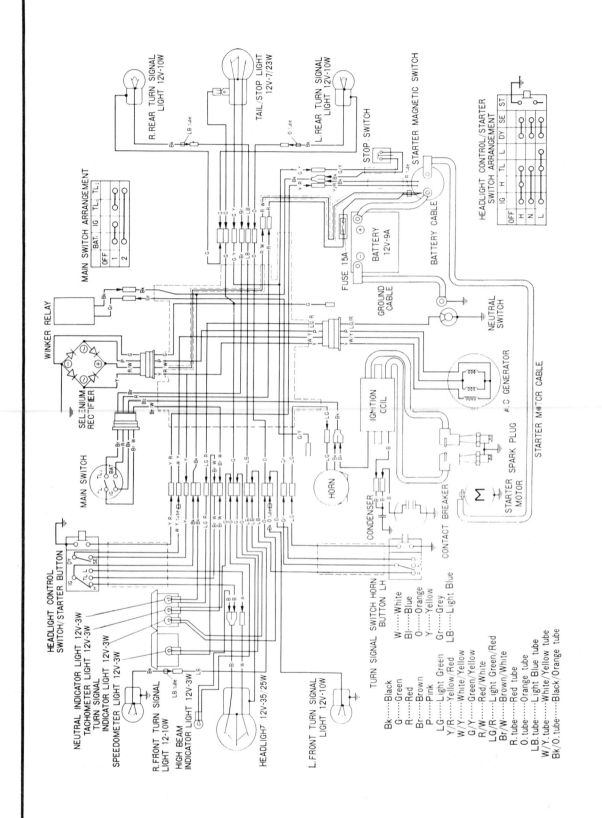

Fig 6.2 WIRING DIAGRAM: CB175 - GENERAL EXPORT TYPE

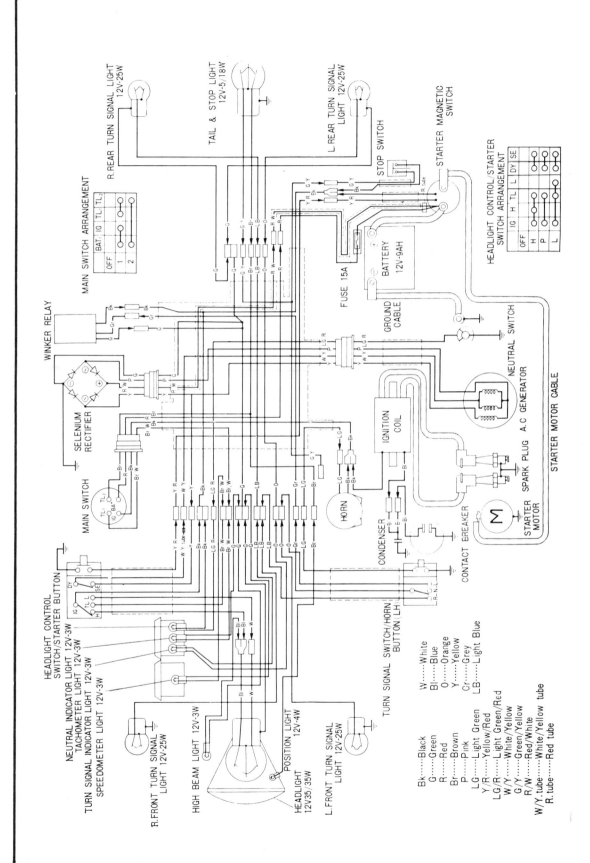

Fig 6.3 WIRING DIAGRAM: CB175 - UK TYPE

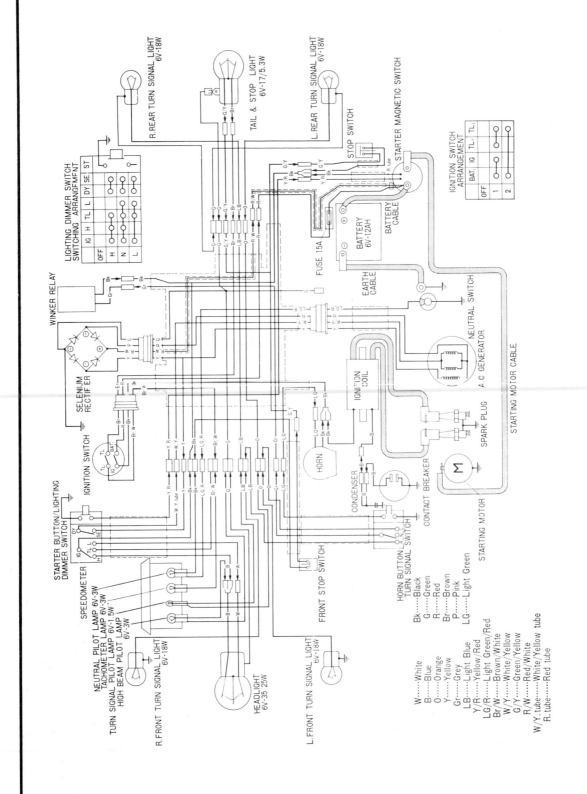

Fig 6.4 WIRING DIAGRAM: CD175 - USA TYPE

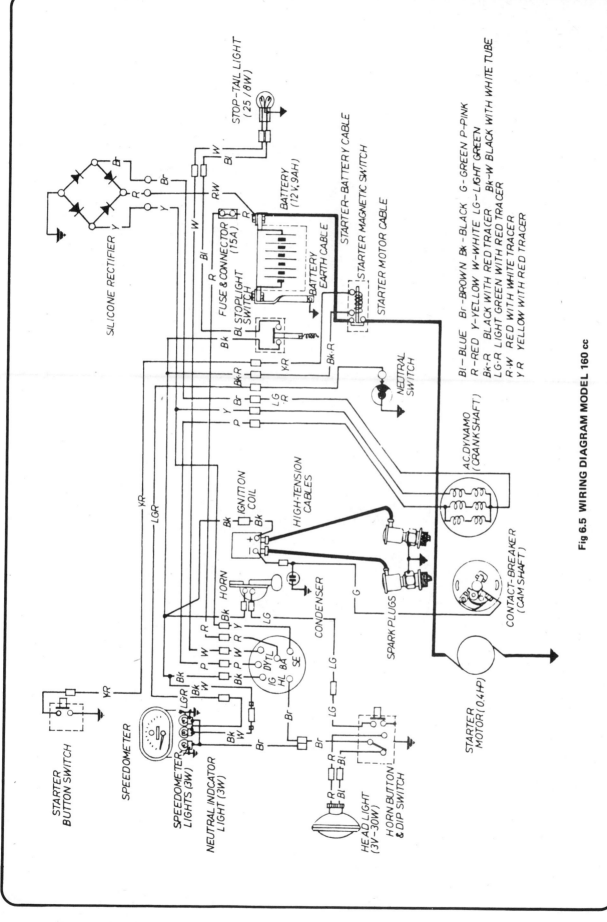

Fig 6.5 WIRING DIAGRAM MODEL 160 cc

The Honda CB 200

Chapter 7 Supplement covering CB 200

Contents

Specifications: CB 200 model

Engine:

Type	Parallel twin cylinder, inclined at 8° from the vertical, 180° crankshaft, single overhead camshaft
Bore	55.5 mm
Bore wear limit	55.6 mm
Stroke	41.0 mm
Cubic capacity	198 cc
Compression ratio	9.0 : 1
Maximum BHP	17 @ 9,000 rpm

Piston and rings ...

Piston and rings	Two compression rings, one oil control ring
Oversizes	0.25, 0.50, 0.75, 1.00 mm
Ring end gap - all rings	0.006 - 0.014 in. (0.15 - 0.35 mm)
Ring end gap - wear limit	0.030 in. (0.75 mm)
Ring groove clearance - Top	0.0016 - 0.0030 in. (0.04 - 0.075 mm)
Second	0.0010 - 0.0024 in. (0.025 - 0.06 mm)
Oil	0.0006 - 0.0018 in. (0.015 - 0.045 mm)
Ring groove clearance - wear limit, all rings	0.006 in. (0.15 mm)
Gudgeon pin O.D.	0.5903 - 0.5906 in. (14.994 - 15.000 mm)
Gudgeon pin O.D. - wear limit	0.5866 in. (14.9 mm)
Gudgeon pin hole diameter in piston	0.5906 - 0.5909 in. (15.002 - 15.008 mm)
Gudgeon pin hole diameter in piston - wear limit	0.5925 in. (15.05 mm)

Valves and springs:

Valve seat angle - inlet and exhaust	45°
Valve seat width - inlet and exhaust	0.0394 - 0.0551 in. (1.0 - 1.4 mm)
Valve seat width - inlet and exhaust, wear limit	0.0709 in. (1.8 mm)
Valve stem diameter - Inlet	0.2157 - 0.2161 in. (5.48 - 5.49 mm)
Exhaust	0.2150 - 0.2154 in. (5.46 - 5.472 mm)
Valve stem diameter wear limit - Inlet	0.2134 in. (5.42 mm)
Exhaust	0.2126 in. (5.40 mm)
Valve stem to guide clearance - Inlet	0.006 - 0.0014 in. (0.015 - 0.0235 mm)
Exhaust	0.0013 - 0.0022 in. (0.033 - 0.055 mm)
Valve spring free length - Inner	1.3091 in. (33.25 mm)
Outer	1.3799 in. (35.05 mm)
Valve spring free length - wear limit - Inner	1.2598 in. (32.0 mm)
Outer	1.3583 in. (34.5 mm)
Valve tappet clearance (cold) - Inlet and exhaust ...	-.002 in. (0.05 mm)

Camshaft and rockers:

Cam lobe height -	Inlet	...	...	...	...	...	0.9865 in. (25.058 mm)
	Exhaust	...	...	...	...	...	0.9792 in. (24.972 mm)
Cam lobe height - wear limit	-	Inlet	...	...	...	...	0.9803 in. (24.9 mm)
	-	Exhaust	...	...	...	...	0.9724 in. (24.7 mm)
Rocker arm to shaft clearance	...	...	...	...	...	...	0.0005 - 0.0017 in. (0.013 - 0.043 mm)
Rocker arm to shaft clearance - wear limit	...	...	...	...	0.0039 in. (0.1 mm)

Valve timing:

Inlet valve	-	Opens	...	...	...	...	...	5º B.T.D.C.
		Closes	...	...	...	...	...	35º A.B.D.C.
Exhaust valve	-	Opens	...	...	...	...	...	40º B.B.D.C.
		Closes	...	...	...	...	...	5º A.T.D.C.

Carburettor:

Main jet	...	...	...	...	...	...	...	No. 88
Slow running jet	...	...	...	...	...	...	No. 38
Normal jet needle setting	...	...	...	...	...	Third groove
Pilot air screw setting	...	...	...	...	...	1¼ ± 1/8 turns
Float height *	...	...	...	...	...	...	0.827 in. (21 mm)
Idle speed	...	...	...	...	...	...	1200 rpm

* The float height is taken as the distance between the carburettor body and the opposite edge of the float.

Crankshaft and connecting rods:

Crankshaft run out at centre	... ...	0.0008 in. (0.02 mm)
Crankshaft run out at centre - service limit	... ...	0.0059 in. (0.15 mm)
Connecting rod big end side clearance	... ...	0.0028 - 0.0130 in. (0.07 - 0.33 mm)
Connecting rod big end side clearance - wear limit	... ...	0.0236 in. (0.6 mm)
Connecting rod small end I.D	... ...	0.5912 - 0.5919 in. (15.016 - 15.034 mm)
Connecting rod small end I.D. - wear limit	... ...	0.5933 in. (15.07 mm)

Oil pump:

Pump body to plunger clearance	... ...	0.0010 - 0.0025 in. (0.025 - 0.063 mm)
Pump body to plunger clearance - wear limit	... ...	0.0067 in. (0.17 mm)
Clutch outer to pump rod clearance	... ...	0.0010 - 0.0030 in. (0.025 - 0.075 mm)
Clutch outer to pump rod clearance - wear limit	... ...	0.0059 in. (0.15 mm)

Clutch:

No. of friction plates	... ...	5
No. of plain plates	... ...	5
No. of springs	... ...	4
Friction plate thickness	... ...	0.1150 - 0.1213 in. (2.92 - 3.08 mm)
Friction plate thickness wear limit	... ...	0.1024 in. (2.6 mm)
Clutch plate warpage	... ...	0.0039 in. (0.1 mm)
Clutch plate warpage service limit	... ...	0.0079 in. (0.2 mm)
Clutch spring free length	... ...	1.126 in. (28.26 mm)
Clutch spring free length wear limit	... ...	1.0512 in. (26.7 mm)

Gear ratios:

Primary drive reduction	... ...	3.700
Gear ratio	-	1st	... ...	2.769
		2nd	... ...	1.882
		3rd	... ...	1.5450
		4th	... ...	1.174
		5th	... ...	0.960
Final drive reduction	... ...	2.333

Frame specifications - general:

Front brake drum I.D.	... ...	6.2992 - 6.3110 in. (160 - 160.3 mm)
Front brake drum I.D. - wear limit	... ...	6.3386 in. (161.0 mm)
Rear brake drum I.D.	... ...	5.5118 - 5.5236 in. (140.0 - 140.3 mm)
Rear brake drum I.D. - wear limit	... ...	5.5512 in. (141.0 mm)
Front and rear brake lining thickness	... ...	0.1772 - 0.1850 in. (4.5 - 4.7 mm)
Front brake lining thickness wear limit	... ...	0.0787 in. (2.0 mm)
Rear brake lining thickness wear limit	... ...	0.0591 in. (1.5 mm)
Disc brake face run out (USA)	... ...	0.0020 in. (0.05 mm)
Disc brake face run out wear limit	... ...	0.0079 in. (0.20 mm)
Disc brake warpage (USA)	... ...	0.0020 in. (0.05 mm)
Disc brake warpage service limit	... ...	0.0118 in. (0.3 mm)
Disc brake thickness (USA)	... ...	0.1929 - 0.2008 in. (4.9 - 5.1 mm)
Disc brake thickness - wear limit	... ...	0.1575 in. (4.0 mm)
Front fork spring length	... ...	17.8622 in. (453.7 mm)

Front fork spring length - wear limit ... ... 17.5197 in. (445 mm)
Rear suspension spring length ... ... 7.7441 in. (196.7 mm)
Rear suspension spring length wear limit ... ... 7.2835 in. (185 mm)

Torque wrench settings:	lbs ft	kg cm
Engine:		
Cylinder head (apply oil to nuts before tightening)	13 - 16	180 - 220
Camshaft sprocket bolts	12.3 - 16.6	170 - 230
Tappet adjusting nuts	5.1 - 8.0	70 - 110
Crankcase bolts - 6 mm	5.1 - 8.0	70 - 110
8 mm	14.5 - 18.8	200 - 260
Alternator rotor	25.3 - 32.5	350 - 450
Frame:		
Steering stem nut	57.9 - 72.3	800 - 1000
Top and bottom fork yoke pinch bolts	13.0 - 18.1	180 - 250
Swinging arm pivot bolt	43.4 - 50.6	600 - 700
Front wheel spindle	43.4 - 57.9	600 - 800
Rear wheel spindle	50.6 - 65.1	700 - 900
Brake arm bolts	5.8 - 7.2	80 - 100
Gear lever and kickstart bolts	5.8 - 7.2	80 - 100

Summary
of routine maintenance, adjustments and capacities

Spark plug ... ... NGK D8ES-L or Nippon Denso X24ES

Spark plug gap ... ... 0.024 - 0.028 in. (0.6 - 0.7 mm)

Contact breaker gap ... ... 0.012 - 0.016 in. (0.3 - 0.4 mm)

Valve tappet clearance (cold engine) inlet ... ... 0.002 in. (0.05 mm)
 exhaust ... ... 0.002 in. (0.05 mm)

Tyre pressure - front ... ... 26 psi (1.8 kg/cm^2)
 rear ... ... 28 psi (2.0 kg/cm^2)

Increase rear tyre pressure to 34 psi (2.4 kg/cm^2) when carrying a passenger.

Fuel tank capacity (total) ... ... 1.98 Imp. gal. (9.0 litres)

Fuel tank reserve capacity ... ... 0.55 Imp. gal. (2.5 litres)

Engine/gearbox oil capacity ... ... 3.0 Imp. pt. (1.7 litres)

Front fork leg oil capacity - dry ... ... 128 - 132 cc
 wet ... ... 115 - 118 cc

Recommended lubricants and fuel

Component	Castrol Product	Quantity
Engine/gearbox	Castrol GTX	3 Imp. pints (1.70 litres)
Grease nipples and bearings	Castrol LM grease	
Control cables	Castrol Everyman oil	
Telescopic forks	Castrol TQF	Dry 128 - 132 cc/leg
		Wet 115 - 118 cc/leg
Fuel required	91 octane or higher	

The CB200 model: Comparison with the CB175

The Honda CB200 has been developed from the successful CB175 which itself came from a long line of similar smaller capacity twins. However, unlike its predecessors, the increase in capacity has been obtained by altering both the bore and stroke and not just the bore size. The fifth gear ratio has also been raised. The clutch operating mechanism has been changed, thrust being transferred by means of three ball bearings that are mounted inside the primary drive cover. The oil filler cap has been relocated forward in the primary drive cover. The carburettors are mounted on synthetic rubber manifolds and their choke size has been reduced to 18 mm (cf. 20 mm on the CB175). Access to the centrifugal oil filter is now obtained by removing the whole primary drive cover since an inspection cover is not fitted. Also, instead of two staggered primary drive gears, a single sintered metal gear is fitted. The alternator output has also been increased to 97 watts at 5000 r.p.m. (cf 80 watts).

The frame for the CB200 is the same as that on the CB175 except that the rear footrest and silencer frame loop is of tubular construction and not a pressing. The rear chain size has been increased to 5/8 " x ¼" on the CB200.

On the latest version a disc front brake is fitted, the unusual point being that it is cable operated using a similar type of mechanism as that used to apply thrust to the clutch.

1 Engine unit and cycle parts: Dismantling, examination and reassembly

1   Although the CB200 model is similar in many respects to the CB175 model described in the preceding Chapters, reference should always be made to this Chapter first in view of the need to follow a modified procedure when certain components of the CB200 model have to be removed and replaced. Where no information is given in this Chapter, it can be assumed the procedure is identical to that given for the CB175 model in the earlier Chapters.
2   Routine maintenance procedure closely follows the schedules already described in the earlier Section of this Manual, and is common throughout the Honda range of lightweight twins.

2 Removal and replacement of the cylinder head, camshaft and camshaft chain

1   The camshaft of the CB200 model differs from that of the CB175 in that the sprocket is removable and the camshaft chain is continuous and not joined by a spring link. This effects cylinder head removal and the subsequent reassembly procedure, also the method for timing the valves.
2   Commence by removing the breather tube from the cylinder head cover.
3   Remove the contact breaker points cover and withdraw the screws securing the contact breaker base plate, after having marked the plate so that it can be replaced in exactly the same position (otherwise the ignition timing will have to be reset).
4   Remove the bolt in the end of the camshaft and pull off the auto-advance/retard unit.
5   Remove the left-hand side cover which houses the points.
6   Remove the right-hand side cover, complete with its tachometer drive.
7   Remove the tappet adjusting caps and slacken off the tappet adjusting screws.
8   Remove the eight domed head nuts and lift off the cylinder head cover.
9   Screw a 6 mm bolt into the rocker arm shafts and pull them out. Remove the rocker arms.
10 Loosen the camshaft chain tensioner locking bolt and remove the tension from the chain.
11 Remove the alternator cover and rotate the rotor until one of the camshaft sprocket bolts is at the top, then remove the bolt.

Rotate the rotor one full turn and remove the other bolt. Be careful not to drop either of the bolts down the chain tunnel into the crankcase.
12 Lift the chain off the sprocket and lift out the camshaft and the sprocket from the right-hand side. To stop the chain falling down the tunnel it should be hooked up with a piece of wire.
13 The cylinder head is now free to be lifted off the cylinder block.
14 The camshaft chain can be removed only after the crankcases have been split and the crankshaft removed since no connecting link is fitted.
15 Replace in the reverse order to the above. Reset the valve timing as described in the next Section. Tighten the cylinder head nuts in the sequence shown in the accompanying diagram. Do not forget to lightly grease the tachometer drive and also the auto-advance/retard unit.

3 Valve timing

1   Replace the tensioner pushrod, locking it into the fully pressed home position. Fit a new cylinder head gasket. Hook up the camshaft chain and replaced the cylinder head as described in Section 2.
2   Rotate the crankshaft to align the "T" mark on the alternator rotor with the index mark on the crankcase cover.
3   Install the camshaft chain onto the sprocket so that the matching lines on the sprocket are in alignment with the upper surface of the cylinder head with the dowel pin uppermost.
4   Position the sprocket on the flange of the camshaft with the tachometer drive side cutaway facing upwards and the matching lines horizontal (see diagram accompanying). Tighten both sprocket bolts.
5   Loosen the chain tensioner setting bolt and check that the camshaft chain is properly tensioned and the valve timing is still correct.

4 Valve springs

1   The valve springs are of a dual rate type and when refitting make sure that the narrow pitch end goes next the cylinder head.

5 Piston and piston rings

1   The pistons are marked with an arrow on the top. When replacing them this arrow must point forwards.
2   The piston rings are of different cross section and must not only be fitted into their correct grooves but also the correct way up. The top of the ring is marked with a letter "R" or some other marking. The accompanying diagram shows the correct order of assembly.

6 Clutch operating mechanism and adjustment

1   This is relocated and is now found in the right-hand (primary drive) engine cover. To remove the clutch cable, first remove the inspection cover, then unhook the cable from its operating arm. Remove the cable by unscrewing the adjuster out of the engine cover.
2   To adjust the clutch, first screw the handlebar adjuster right in and also the adjuster in the engine cover so that there is a maximum of free cable. Remove the clutch adjustment inspection cover.
3   Slacken the clutch adjuster locknut. Turn the adjuster screw clockwise until resistance is felt then back off the screw anti-clockwise for a ¼-½ turn. Tighten the lock nut whilst holding the screw in this position.
4   Rotate the cable adjuster in the engine cover until the free

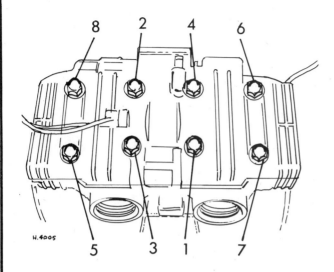

Fig. 7.1. Slackening and tightening sequence for cylinder head bolts

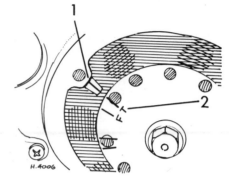

Fig. 7.2a. Valve timing: Aligning the rotor marks

1   Pointer

2   'T' mark on rotor face

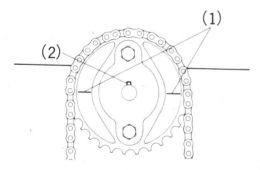

Fig. 7.2b. Valve timing: Aligning the camshaft marks

1   Lines on sprocket

2   Dowel pin in uppermost position

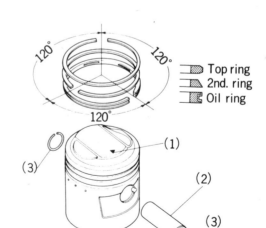

Fig. 7.3. Piston and piston ring assembly

1   Piston crown

2   Gudgeon pin

3   Circlips

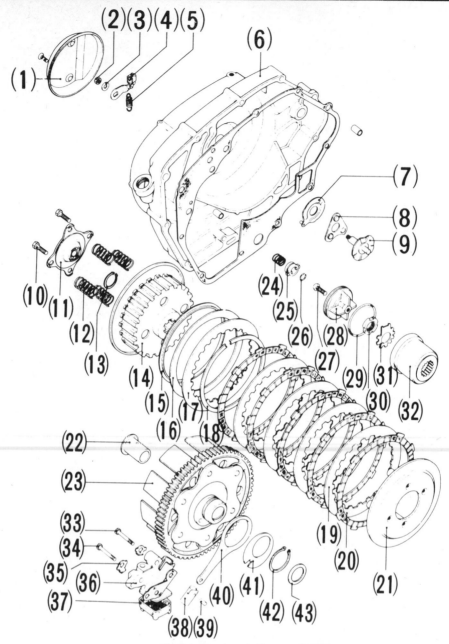

Fig. 7.4. Clutch and oil pump: CB200

1	Clutch adjustment inspection cover		23	Clutch outer
2	Nut 6 mm		24	Oil guide spring
3	Washer		25	Oil guide
4	Clutch lever		26	Circlip
5	Clutch lever return spring		27	Screw 6 mm
6	Right-hand side engine cover		28	Oil filter cap
7	Clutch camplate		29	'O' ring
8	Thrust ballbearings and retainer		30	Locknut
9	Clutch operating cam		31	Lock washer
10	Bolt 6 mm		32	Oil filter rotor
11	Clutch thrust plate		33	Bolt 6 mm
12	Clutch spring		34	Bolt 6 mm
13	Circlip		35	Lock washer
14	Clutch centre		36	Oil pump
15	Disc spring seat		37	Oil filter screen
16	Disc spring		38	Pump plunger
17	Spacing clutch plate		39	Pump plunger connecting pin
18	Circlip		40	Pump operating rod
19	Plain clutch plate		41	Pump rod side washer
20	Friction clutch plate		42	Circlip
21	Clutch pressure plate		43	Thrust washer
22	Collar			

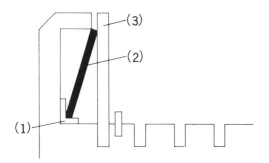

Fig. 7.5. Correct location of clutch disc spring

1   Clutch disc spring seat   2   Clutch disc spring

play measured at the end of the handlebar lever is 0.4-0.8" (10 - 20 mm). Tighten the locknut and slide the rubber cover over the adjuster.
5   Further fine adjustment can be made at the handlebar lever.

7   The clutch: construction

1   Refer to the line drawing for the clutch component details. Note that there is no transfer clutch thrust pushrod since the operating cable is on the right-hand side and not on the left as for the CB175.
2   When reassembling the clutch be sure to correctly position the clutch disc spring, as per the accompanying diagram.

8   Right-hand engine cover: Removal

1   The clutch cable has first to be removed, as described in Section 6.

9   Centrifugal oil filter

1   To clean or gain access to the centrifugal oil filter the right hand engine cover has to be removed. See Section. Pull out the oil filter cap by using an 8 mm bolt screwed into the hole provided.

10   Primary drive gear

1   Only a single gear is fitted (cf. Two separate, staggered, gears in the CB175). This can be lifted off the crankshaft once the centrifugal oil filter has been removed (the clutch outer has also only a single gear to mesh with the crankshaft primary gear).

11   Gear cluster

1   Although the gear cluster is of the same type and assembly as the CB175 the fifth gear ratio has been changed and thus the

number of teeth on these gears are different. The CB200 has 24 teeth on the main shaft and layshaft fifth gear pinion (cf 25 Teeth on CB175).

12   Handlebar clamps

The handlebar clamps are marked at the front with a punch mark. If the clamps are separated in order to remove the handlebars, it is important that the upper clamps are replaced with the punch mark facing the front of the machine.

13   Front wheel spindle and clamps

1   When refitting the front wheel, the clamps at the lower end of the fork legs must be replaced so that there is no gap at the front when the nuts are tightened. To aid refitting, the clamps have an embossed 'F' to denote the forward facing end and also an arrow, which must point in a forward direction.
2   When the front wheel spindle is refitted, the nut and split pin must be on the left-hand side of the machine.
3   Check the three bolts that retain the disc brake caliper (if fitted) at regular intervals. They have been known to work loose and are occasionally found slack on a new machine if they have been slackened to aid the fitting of the front wheel and have then been overlooked.

14   Front wheel disc brake

1   Late models are fitted with a disc brake that is operated by cable. The cable actuates a quick thread worm within the brake caliper assembly and it is this that presses the pads against the disc when the brake is applied.
2   The pads can be removed without need to separate the caliper unit, after the front wheel has been removed. Each pad has a locating tab; the pad will lift out of the housing for examination and replacement, if necessary.
3   Each pad has a red tab which denotes the limit of wear. When this point is reached, the pad must be renewed. Always renew pads as a pair, never singly.
4   It is rarely necessary to remove the disc, but if this should be required, it will be found that the disc is bolted to the hub by means of six bolts and tab washers. The hub of the disc brake models is of slightly different construction to permit mounting of the disc and has an alternative speedometer drive arrangement.

15   Front brake stop lamp switch

A micro-switch is attached to the front brake lever so that the rear stop lamp will light when the front brake is applied. The switch acts on the plunger principle, the plunger extending as the brake lever is operated. It is a self-contained unit attached to the front brake lever and must be replaced as such, should it malfunction.

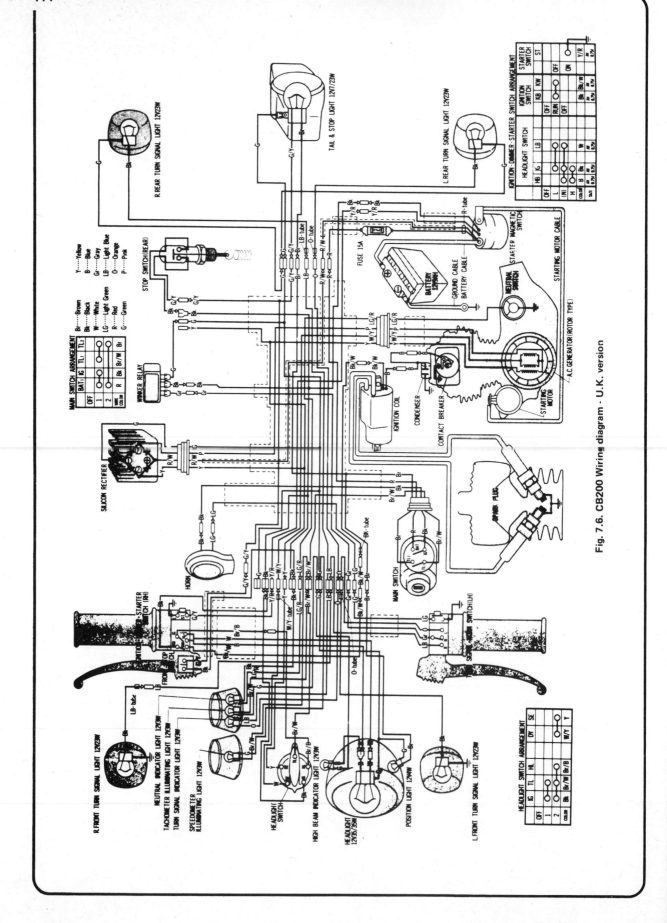

Fig. 7.6. CB200 Wiring diagram - U.K. version

Index

Metric conversion tables

Inches	Decimals	Millimetres	Millimetres to Inches		Inches to Millimetres	
			mm	Inches	Inches	mm
1/64	0.015625	0.3969	0.01	0.00039	0.001	0.0254
1/32	0.03125	0.7937	0.02	0.00079	0.002	0.0508
3/64	0.046875	1.1906	0.03	0.00118	0.003	0.0762
1/16	0.0625	1.5875	0.04	0.00157	0.004	0.1016
5/64	0.078125	1.9844	0.05	0.00197	0.005	0.1270
3/32	0.09375	2.3812	0.06	0.00236	0.006	0.1524
7/64	0.109375	2.7781	0.07	0.00276	0.007	0.1778
1/8	0.125	3.1750	0.08	0.00315	0.008	0.2032
9/64	0.140625	3.5719	0.09	0.00354	0.009	0.2286
5/32	0.15625	3.9687	0.1	0.00394	0.01	0.254
11/64	0.171875	4.3656	0.2	0.00787	0.02	0.508
3/16	0.1875	4.7625	0.3	0.01181	0.03	0.762
13/64	0.203125	5.1594	0.4	0.01575	0.04	1.016
7/32	0.21875	5.5562	0.5	0.01969	0.05	1.270
15/64	0.234375	5.9531	0.6	0.02362	0.06	1.524
1/4	0.25	6.3500	0.7	0.02756	0.07	1.778
17/64	0.265625	6.7469	0.8	0.03150	0.08	2.032
9/32	0.28125	7.1437	0.9	0.03543	0.09	2.286
19/64	0.296875	7.5406	1	0.03937	0.1	2.54
5, 16	0.3125	7.9375	2	0.07874	0.2	5.08
21/64	0.328125	8.3344	3	0.11811	0.3	7.62
11/32	0.34375	8.7312	4	0.15748	0.4	10.16
23/64	0.359375	9.1281	5	0.19685	0.5	12.70
3/8	0.375	9.5250	6	0.23622	0.6	15.24
25/64	0.390625	9.9219	7	0.27559	0.7	17.78
13/32	0.40625	10.3187	8	0.31496	0.8	20.32
27/64	0.421875	10.7156	9	0.35433	0.9	22.86
7/16	0.4375	11.1125	10	0.39370	1	25.4
29/64	0.453125	11.5094	11	0.43307	2	50.8
15/32	0.46875	11.9062	12	0.47244	3	76.2
31/64	0.484375	12.3031	13	0.51181	4	101.6
1/2	0.5	12.7000	14	0.55118	5	127.0
33/64	0.515625	13.0969	15	0.59055	6	152.4
17/32	0.53125	13.4937	16	0.62992	7	177.8
35/64	0.546875	13.8906	17	0.66929	8	203.2
9/16	0.5625	14.2875	18	0.70866	9	228.6
37/64	0.578125	14.6844	19	0.74803	10	254.0
19/32	0.59375	15.0812	20	0.78740	11	279.4
39/64	0.609375	15.4781	21	0.82677	12	304.8
5/8	0.625	15.8750	22	0.86614	13	330.2
41/64	0.640625	16.2719	23	0.90551	14	355.6
21/32	0.65625	16.6687	24	0.94488	15	381.0
43/64	0.671875	17.0656	25	0.98425	16	406.4
11/16	0.6875	17.4625	26	1.02362	17	431.8
45/64	0.703125	17.8594	27	1.06299	18	457.2
23/32	0.71875	18.2562	28	1.10236	19	482.6
47/64	0.734375	18.6531	29	1.14173	20	508.0
3/4	0.75	19.0500	30	1.18110	21	533.4
49/64	0.765625	19.4469	31	1.22047	22	558.8
25/32	0.78125	19.8437	32	1.25984	23	584.2
51/64	0.796875	20.2406	33	1.29921	24	609.6
13/16	0.8125	20.6375	34	1.33858	25	635.0
53/64	0.828125	21.0344	35	1.37795	26	660.4
27/32	0.84375	21.4312	36	1.41732	27	685.8
55/64	0.859375	21.8281	37	1.4567	28	711.2
7/8	0.875	22.2250	38	1.4961	29	736.6
57/64	0.890625	22.6219	39	1.5354	30	762.0
29/32	0.90625	23.0187	40	1.5748	31	787.4
59/64	0.921875	23.4156	41	1.6142	32	812.8
15/16	0.9375	23.8125	42	1.6535	33	838.2
61/64	0.953125	24.2094	43	1.6929	34	863.6
31/32	0.96875	24.6062	44	1.7323	35	889.0
63/64	0.984375	25.0031	45	1.7717	36	914.4

Metric conversion tables

1   Imperial gallon = 8 Imp pints = 1.16 US gallons = 277.42 cu in = 4.5459 litres

1   US gallon = 4 US quarts = 0.862 Imp gallon = 231 cu in = 3.785 litres

1   Litre = 0.2199 Imp gallon = 0.2642 US gallon = 61.0253 cu in = 1000 cc

Miles to Kilometres		Kilometres to Miles	
1	1.61	1	0.62
2	3.22	2	1.24
3	4.83	3	1.86
4	6.44	4	2.49
5	8.05	5	3.11
6	9.66	6	3.73
7	11.27	7	4.35
8	12.88	8	4.97
9	14.48	9	5.59
10	16.09	10	6.21
20	32.19	20	12.43
30	48.28	30	18.64
40	64.37	40	24.85
50	80.47	50	31.07
60	96.56	60	37.28
70	112.65	70	43.50
80	128.75	80	49.71
90	144.84	90	55.92
100	160.93	100	62.14

lb f ft to Kg f m		Kg f m to lb f ft		lb f/in^2 : Kg f/cm^2		Kg f/cm^2 : lb f/in^2	
1	0.138	1	7.233	1	0.07	1	14.22
2	0.276	2	14.466	2	0.14	2	28.50
3	0.414	3	21.699	3	0.21	3	42.67
4	0.553	4	28.932	4	0.28	4	56.89
5	0.691	5	36.165	5	0.35	5	71.12
6	0.829	6	43.398	6	0.42	6	85.34
7	0.967	7	50.631	7	0.49	7	99.56
8	1.106	8	57.864	8	0.56	8	113.79
9	1.244	9	65.097	9	0.63	9	128.00
10	1.382	10	72.330	10	0.70	10	142.23
20	2.765	20	144.660	20	1.41	20	284.47
30	4.147	30	216.990	30	2.11	30	426.70

Printed by
Haynes Publishing Group
Sparkford Yeovil Somerset
England